PENGUIN BOOKS

THE RETURN OF THE NAKED CHEF

'There's only one Jamie Oliver. Great to watch. Great to cook'
Delia Smith

'The recipes are gorgeous – in particular, composed salads such as
mozzarella and grilled chilli, or seared carpaccio of beef with beetroot,
horseradish, watercress and parmesan' *New Statesman*

'He makes it all look so easy, damn him' *Evening Standard*

'The design and photography are clear and luscious and the recipes are the kind
you want to try and really can make at home' *Time Out*

'First class … accessible easy meals to impress your friends with but which
won't take for ever to make' *Guardian*

'He's the hottest thing in the kitchen since chilli peppers. We just can't seem to
get enough of Jamie Oliver' *Evening Standard*

'From salads to roasts, desserts to pasta, he has created a foolproof repertoire
of simple, feisty and delicious recipes which combine bold flavours with fresh
ingredients. At the same time he avoids culinary jargon and any complicated
time-consuming processes … unpretentious, charismatic, streetwise and
passionate about food'
Food and Wine Magazine

'Simply delicious' *Mail on Sunday*

ABOUT THE AUTHOR

Jamie Oliver grew up in his parents' country pub, the Cricketers in Clavering, where he started cooking at the age of eight, before studying at London's Westminster Catering College. He then went on to work with some of the top chefs in the country – namely Antonio Carluccio at the Neal Street Restaurant and Rose Gray and Ruth Rogers at the River Café. He is now running the restaurant at Monte's in Knightsbridge, London. He writes regularly for *The Times* magazine on Saturday and is the Food Editor at *Marie Claire*. He is the author of two other books published by Penguin, *The Naked Chef* and *Happy Days with the Naked Chef*.

Jamie is twenty-six and lives in London with his lovely wife, Jools.

Jamie Oliver
the return of the Naked Chef

PENGUIN BOOKS

to my missus . . .

sorry,

the lovely Jools x

PENGUIN BOOKS

Published by the Penguin Group
Penguin Books Ltd, 80 Strand, London WC2R 0RL, England
Penguin Putnam Inc., 375 Hudson Street, New York, New York 10014, USA
Penguin Books Australia Ltd, 250 Camberwell Road, Camberwell, Victoria 3124, Australia
Penguin Books Canada Ltd, 10 Alcorn Avenue, Toronto, Ontario, Canada M4V 3B2
Penguin Books India (P) Ltd, 11 Community Centre, Panchsheel Park,
New Delhi – 110 017, India
Penguin Books (NZ) Ltd, Cnr Rosedale and Airborne Roads,
Albany, Auckland, New Zealand
Penguin Books (South Africa) (Pty) Ltd, 24 Sturdee Avenue,
Rosebank 2196, South Africa

Penguin Books Ltd, Registered Offices: 80 Strand, London WC2R 0RL, England

www.penguin.com

First published by Michael Joseph 2000
Published in Penguin Books 2002
1

Set in Helvetica Neue Light
Printed in England by Butler & Tanner, Frome, Somerset

contents

10 introduction

14 make life easy

16 potty about herbs

20 morning glory

36 tapas, munchies and snacks

52 simple salads and dressings

82 soups and broths

94 pasta and risotto

146 fish and shellfish

170 meat, poultry and game

198 vegetables

220 bread

238 desserts

262 bevvies

274 stocks, sauces, bits, bobs, this, that and the other

279 index

286 thanks, nice one, shout going out, cheers, respect

introduction

Blimey, what a year! If I had been told a year and a half ago that I would be sitting here now writing my second book as a follow-up to *The Naked Chef* I would never have believed it. Having the chance to write the first was amazing, but to be allowed another crack of the whip is just superb. And am I ready for it? Yes, surrounded by the pukka people at Penguin, good friends and family, you better believe it. I'm gagging for it!

As you can imagine, being the youngest chef on the block, having a bestselling book as well as a cracking television series, not to mention being a bit scruffy and coming from Essex, I have come in for quite a bit of stick from folk. I don't mind. In fact, I quite enjoy it. It makes me laugh. This book isn't about cheffy food, it's for normal people who want shortcuts and tips; people who want to make simple day-to-day meals different and absolutely fantastic or something a little bit more fruity and indulgent. At the end of the day, it's for everyone who is interested in cooking tasty, gutsy, simple, commonsense food and having a right good laugh at the same time. That's what food's all about. It's not just about eating. To me it's about passing the potatoes around the table, ripping up some bread, licking my fingers, getting tipsy and enjoying the company of good friends or family. Pass us the mustard, Dad.

The response to *The Naked Chef* from the media and
thought that I would have been asked to cook at No. 10 for
meeting? What a great buzz that was. Or hearing Zoë Bal
tuna for dinner? Can't get better than that. Or having Mrs
I'm washing my hair. And some of the letters I received
saying they've cooked from the book for the in-laws in dodgy

There was one occasion when I thought I would have to
of the road shouted out, 'Oi, you, Naked! Come 'ere. I want
me, I waited for him to walk over, only for him to say in ar
kitchen three nights a week cos my missus says if that
weeks if I'd a seen ya, I'd a knocked your 'ead off.' Then his
it. I think I'm a good chef. So thanks mate, respect.' And
bill.' And then there were the old ladies in Sheffield – righ'
said, 'OK love, sign us this book here. Make sure there's
and we love your lingo, don't we, Gwenda?' 'Yes, yes, we do
you with your clothes on. Can't you get your kit off?' Now
like a beetroot. I wanted to say something smart back bu'

I've spoken to loads of strangers while shopping in the
me constructive feedback. This has probably taught me the
massively influenced my approach to this book. Yeah, I stil
Naked Chef: using the *bare* essentials of your larder and
But I'm also keen to make use of new ingredients which are
and pulses to fresh herbs and oils from different regions o
quality will definitely improve. PS Check out the index where

the public has been absolutely fantastic. Who would have
Tony Blair and the Italian prime minister at their summit
on the radio say that she'd cooked Fatboy Slim my seared
Merton offer me her baked pasta recipe? Not today love,
were fantastic. It's amazing getting a letter from someone
situations and scored massive brownie points. God bless ya.
eg it, because some bloomin' great geezer over the other side
a word.' Holding on to my vitals, with my life flashing before
aggressive voice, 'Thanks to you mate, I'm in the bleedin'
blond young boy can do it, so can you. For the first couple of
voice softened and he said, 'I really enjoy it now I've got into
said, 'Thanks mate. All the best. I'll send you the laundry
tigers they were. While constantly patting my bottom they
kisses on it. Now, we love your programme, we love your book
Maureen. Pukka, wicked it is. But we're a bit surprised to see
don't get embarrassed easily, but these OAPs had me blushing
every time I opened my mouth I sounded like Scooby-Doo.
supermarkets and walking down the street who have given
most about what real people at home really want and it has
believe in the two things that resulted in my name of the
stripping down restaurant methods to the reality of home.
now being stocked in your average supermarket, from fruits
the world. If we all support these ingredients then variety and
you'll find the V sign pointing out the vegetarian recipes.

make life easy

Before you start cooking, I can't stress enough how much every kitchen should be
stocked with the basics. Do this once and get it done properly instead of buying bits
and pieces. Buy the ingredients listed below, which I promise won't cost you the earth
and will keep you in good stead for the coming year.

cupboard stuff

spices

fresh stuff

cont...
rice : basmati, risotto (Arborio or Camaroli)
capers : salted
olives : black and green
soy sauce
fish sauce
oyster sauce
tinned whole peeled plum tomatoes
sun-dried tomatoes (dried or in oil)
dried mushrooms (porcini)
chocolate : good quality cooking (70% cocoa
              solids)
cocoa powder (70% chocolate)
spices

Black peppercorns
Dried chillies
Nutmeg
Cloves
Coriander seeds
Fennel seeds
Cumin seeds.
Caraway seeds
Fenugreek seeds

a bowl of lemor
a couple of lim
garlic
ginger
onions and
chillies
potatoes
herbs

cupboard stuff

- Oils: extra virgin olive, olive, sunflower
- Vinegars: red wine, white wine, balsamic, rice wine
- Mustards: Dijon, wholegrain, English
- Salt: Maldon sea, table, cooking
- Sugar: brown, white, icing
- Flour: plain, self-raising, strong pasta (fine strong) Tipo '00', corn
- Baking powder, bicarbonate of soda
- Semolina, couscous
- Dried pasta: spaghetti, linguine, tagliatelle, penne, farfalle
- Pulses (dried or tinned): borlotti, cannellini, flageolet and butter beans, yellow split peas, lentils, chickpeas
- Rice: long-grain pilaf, basmati, Arborio or Carnaroli risotto rice
- Anchovies in olive oil or salt
- Capers: salted (small ones are best)
- Olives: black, green
- Soy sauce, fish sauce, oyster sauce
- Tinned whole peeled plum tomatoes, sun-dried tomatoes (dried or in oil)
- Dried mushrooms: porcini
- Chocolate, cocoa powder: good-quality 70% cocoa solids

fresh stuff

Obviously fresh stuff is perishable but there are still some basic things that you will always use. I try to have these ingredients available all the time (see opposite list).

spices

Spices are a must (see opposite). They're non-perishable and they're generally as cheap as chips. The fact that an essential spice and flavouring from a certain part of the world can be kept in your kitchen just waiting to be used is fantastic. By lightly roasting and/or pounding, the spices come alive in smell and flavour. There are classic combinations involved in curries, stews and seasonings, but just a single spice with salt and pepper and a little olive oil can turn an ordinary piece of fish or meat into a more classy, subtle and interesting meal. Generally, I prefer to go to small ethnic shops for my spices, as they tend to be better produced, sourced and stored. And they're a hell of a lot cheaper than your supermarkets or delis.

make life easy

potty about herbs

I'm mad about herbs — so much so that I actually have dreams about seeing big patches of them and feeling the utmost pleasure at having them right there at my culinary disposal (how weird). They're an absolute must for any kitchen, whether at home or in a restaurant. I split fresh herbs up into two sections: *hardy* herbs and *delicate* herbs. Here's my advice for getting them at their best and cheapest.

fresh herbs

hardy herbs

I'm not a gardener, and I certainly haven't got green fingers, but having grown a selection of rosemary, bay, thymes, sages, marjoram, oregano and mint in window-boxes and pots over the last six years, I reckon I've had enough experience to tell you that it's so cheap and dead easy to do. It doesn't matter where you live, or how much space you've got — I've only ever had a garden once (the rest of the time it's been window-boxes for me) and even then I found that potted herbs suited me best. Just spending £15 or so on a selection of herbs will give you an exciting range of flavours and you'll have them right there at your disposal — just with a snip of your scissors. So here's how to pot them, bearing in mind that you don't have to pot from seeds:

- *From seed*

Simply scatter your chosen seeds over some good organic soil in a seed tray. Place them somewhere warm and sunny, and keep them watered. When they have sprouted to about 2.5cm/1 inch high, transfer the seedlings into small pots.

- *Small pot*

Obviously the ideal place to grow your seedlings to the size of the classic market- or shop-bought herb is a greenhouse, but a south-facing window-sill will serve just as well. Good soil, good drainage and a small, but consistent, amount of water every other day will ensure a hardy, tasty baby herb, ready to be planted outside.

- *Transplanting*

  You can buy herbs ready for planting in the garden or you can use your own baby herbs grown from seed (see page 16). Carefully remove the herb plant from its pot and transplant it into your garden, window-box, hanging baskets or large terracotta pots. Make sure you scatter a layer of stones on the bottom of the planting hole, then some good organic soil, before putting the plant on top. This will ensure good drainage. The larger the amount of soil around the herb, the bigger the plant will grow, so bear this in mind.

  When transplanting herbs I tend to use the bigger, more substantial ones like rosemary, bay and sage to shape a bed or pot. The gaps can be filled in with thymes, marjoram and oregano – all are ideal. Mint spreads itself around like mad, and might be better in a pot on its own.

  If you think your herbs need moving to a larger pot or space in your garden at any time, then feel free to do this.

- *Picking and pests*

  Try to pick the new shoots, to encourage the plant into more growth and fullness. Herbs such as oregano and mint tend to die back in cold weather but they grow back with a vengeance in the warmer half of the year. Grow camomile and yarrow near your herbs to keep them healthy, and deter slugs with crushed glass or Vaseline-smeared pot rims. To get rid of aphids, add a small amount of detergent to some water in a watering-can and use this at the first sign of trouble (make sure you wash your herbs thoroughly before using them).

delicate herbs

Quite frankly, I've never had success with growing delicate herbs like parsley, basil, coriander and tarragon. You need a good amount of nutritious soil in a sheltered, light part of the garden, which I've never had (aah), and they will only last for the summer. Lots of my friends have had success using large pots inside the kitchen on a bright window-sill, but I'm far too impatient so I just buy nice big bunches from the market.

dried herbs

Two scenarios here:

1. The herbs are doing so well they've gone mad and are nicking too much space in the garden or pot, so I have to be brutal and cut back the guilty ones to let the others breathe. I then simply bunch up the bits I've cut back, tie them together and hang them up to dry in a warm place (near a boiler, in an airing cupboard, above an oven or just by some hot pipes). They will take about a week to dry out completely.

2. I've bought too many herbs from the market or supermarket and I've only used half. I'm not going to be cooking for the next day or two, so I lay them out on a tray and put them in a warm place. Leave them out near the washing machine or something that generates a little bit of heat. Delicate herbs take anything from a day to a week to dry completely and they have so much more flavour and character than your dried sawdusty herbs in packets. Once dried they can be stored in airtight containers for months.

morning glory

ben

me

I grew up with a mother who cooked us breakfast every single morning, whether it was an unbeatable bacon sarnie, the full monty or her homemade jam and thick-cut bread. She was a star. Now looking back I can really appreciate how well looked after I was, especially when I compare myself to other friends who just got given a couple of Shreddies and some semi-skimmed. 'Breakfast – it's the most important meal of the day,' is what she used to say. My mother was never a worrier but I think she felt a sense of relief if she sent me out the door with a good breakfast inside me because she knew that whatever else happened, I wouldn't starve for the day. She also used to say that your brain needs feeding and that it is at its most effective from seven until eleven in the morning. I'm sure she's right but it didn't do me any good. I still failed miserably at everything apart from art and geology at school, and career-wise I couldn't really see myself as an artistic geologist – all that paint and mud, ooh no.

I think breakfast is one of the most outrageously underrated luxuries in the whole world. Even London as it stands, with its wide variety of restaurants, still offers very little in the way of breakfast. Instead of meetings over lunch or dinner, why not meetings over breakfast? Instead of greasy plastic chairs, why not airy, spacious, fresh and classy diners that serve breakfast from six in the morning until midday? Blooming fantastic, I'd be there. Instead of ingredients bought from the nearest cash and carry, with their classic vacuum-packed bacon and battery eggs, why not a great variety of dry-cured, thick-cut organic bacon and beautiful, golden, free-range eggs from our farmers? After all, there are some that are still doing it properly – it's just a matter of finding them. Fresh juices, self-composed mueslis and homemade breads. I should open up a breakfast diner now before anyone else does – I'd clean up!

The idea of this chapter is not necessarily to make you or your family start eating breakfast every morning. But quite frankly, after a week's work, when the old Saturday and Sunday mornings come along, you don't always have the imagination or the foresight to knock up a quick bit of interesting brekkie for yourself, your family or your partner. If you're after some brownie points and you're a bloke I would highly suggest breakfast in bed for the missus to give you a lucky day, and if you're like my missus, sorry, the lovely Jules, you should attempt a little bit of brekkie for your fella before asking him for a bit of cash for that dress that you've seen in Top Shop. But seriously, before Women's Lib get on the phone, I have so many fantastic memories of breakfast with buddies and I think you'll find some interesting and different things to add to your brekkie repertoire in this chapter. If you know where Pop Tarts originated from then let me know and I'll be over to have some serious words . . . I think it must be in Essex somewhere.

bacon sarnie my stylie

Simple, you may think, but a good bacon sarnie has challenged many chefs, hotels and greasy spoons around the country for years and years. There is a key to this recipe and in my view this is the way to do it.

You need the best dry-cured bacon you can get hold of. This generally means you won't get the shrinkage and watery residue from cooking like you do with most bacon these days. Shame, as we British folk used to be extremely good at rearing and curing good bacon. Second, I would suggest that you try to get hold of thicker-cut bacon; not the wafer-thin stuff that became fashionable a few years ago — you need something you can really get your teeth into. Third, I buy a small, fresh sandwich loaf (gotta be white unless you need your roughage), which should be around 25cm/10 inches long. I then cunningly and politely ask the baker to slice it lengthways, instead of across as normal. I do this all the time and it's great. It's purely a visual thing but it seems to make it taste better to me — I don't know why. I've always been a strange boy.

So, you've got your bacon and your bread. You could quite easily go ahead and cook your bacon and toast your bread under the grill. Lovely. But if you fancy yourself as a bit of a tiger then acquire a ridged griddle pan, which I get as hot as possible (about 4 minutes on the highest heat) and then begin to grill about 4 slices of bacon (per person if you're greedy likc mc). After about 1 minute you can turn the bacon over and it will be golden with those funky charred marks across which I also think benefit the flavour slightly. Cook the other side for 1 more minute. At this point I shuffle all the bacon up one end of the pan to carry on cooking a little longer while I toast off my 2 long pieces of bread in the pan. What I love about this way of doing it is that the bread soaks up just a little (not a lot) of the fat that has cooked out of the bacon which makes it even more tasty. When it has toasted on both sides you could butter your toast — I don't bother — and lay your bacon across each slice. Squeeze the 2 bits of bread together. Now it's ready to be eaten, preferably with some HP sauce. In the past I have also added halved tomatoes and mushrooms to the pan, which do go down very well in the sarnie too.

midnight pan-cooked breakfast

Me and this dish go back a long way. To the pre-shaving days of being an under-age drinker down the Wagon and Horses in Saffron Walden with a fake ID and all my village mates. Only once in a while of course. But seriously, without trying to sound like a lagered-up geezer, I think everyone's experienced the need for food around midnight, whether the binge was small or large, otherwise why would kebab shops be so popular in Britain? Anyway, I always used to have three or four friends back to my house for munchies or to stay the night and this dish was devised so we didn't have too much trouble making it or too much washing up to do. In actual fact, I only had to wipe the non-stick pan clean. It also makes its way from the pan to the plate quite quickly, as patience isn't a virtue at that time of night with my mates!

First of all get the biggest non-stick pan available, and preheat it on a high heat while you gather your ingredients. Obviously you wouldn't be organized at this point so it's a matter of using what you've got, but ideally I like to have mushrooms, bacon, tomatoes, sausages and eggs. By the time you have got these together the pan will be hot, so slice your sausages in half lengthways and pat them out flat so they cook quickly. Place into the pan at one side. On the other side, put a tiny lug of oil and place a pile of mushrooms over it which you can rip up or leave whole. Shake the pan about a bit to coat the mushrooms and season with some salt and pepper. Push to one side and then lay some slices of bacon and halved tomatoes in the pan. Cook for a couple more minutes until the bacon is crisp and golden. Shake the pan and turn the bacon over. Now is the time to put a round of toast in the toaster.

At this stage you should respect the rustic and authentic look and shuffle everything about so that it's all mixed together and add 2 or 3 eggs at different ends of the pan. The whites of the eggs will dribble in and around the sausages, bacon, tomatoes and mushrooms. Turn the heat down a little and continue to cook for another minute before placing the pan under the grill and finishing the eggs to your liking. Using a non-stick pan I've always found the removal of this dish to the plate extremely easy — it will resemble a frisbee and will slide on to your plate with no trouble at all. Doesn't that sound appetizing? But honestly, it really is a gem.

figs, honey and ricotta

I first had this in Florence for brekkie and my initial reaction, as the unworldly person that I am, was why am I having cheese for breakfast? But this combination of perfect figs and honey is amazing, different and damn tasty.

Before you say you don't like figs ... that's what I used to say, remembering chewing on tough, tasteless old figs that you would have to peel the skin off. But I have been converted because the shops and supermarkets are starting to get hold of really good fresh figs, both green and purple. Slightly firm on the outside, soft and sometimes sticky in the middle, with an amazing sweet taste – unlike anything else.

There's no point in me giving you amounts for this recipe as, quite frankly, you can have as much or as little as you like. Myself, I normally go along the 1 fig per person vibe. Score a criss-cross across the top of the fig to about half-way down, then gently squeeze the base of the fig. It will pucker up and look extremely funky, and helps us by exposing a little of the inside which we can dribble honey in. Place the fig beside a slice of fresh ricotta from the deli counter at the supermarket. Dribble the fig and the cheese generously with your favourite honey and tuck in. I have been known to squash both the ricotta and the fig with a fork on to some buttered toast – tuck into that as well, it's all good stuff.

beef tomatoes, basil, ham and mild cheese on thick toast

This is something my dad used to make me on holidays in Cyprus from the hotel's self-service breakfast bar. I've finally found a purpose for the good old beef tomato – for this recipe they are fantastic.

This brekkie or snack takes precisely 1 minute to make. So in go 2 slices of thick bread to the toaster. While toasting, you need to slice your tomatoes as thick as you like, get out a couple of small sprigs of basil, some sliced ham, which I like to remove the fat from, and some mild cheese. Out comes your hot toast. Place it on a plate and very lightly rub it with a garlic clove sliced in half (it's a gesture and it's breakfast, so don't go OTT but it's well worth doing). Then drizzle with some good olive oil – you could butter it if you fancy but I think olive oil keeps in with the Mediterranean thing. Then simply place on your tomatoes – very important, season now with sea salt and freshly ground black pepper. Rip over your basil. Lay on your ham and cheese and tuck in. Very simple, very tasty.

PS A nice poached free-range egg on top does the trick if you've got the extra time.

pukkolla

Pukkolla is my name for this outrageously scrumptious concoction. It's one of the best things you can have for breakfast as it's got everything you need to kickstart your day. Basically it's a bastardized, personally composed muesli. The great thing about it is that you can adjust it to your own preference. It's very handy to have a large plastic airtight container to store your composed pukkolla in, so try and get hold of one.

composing and preserving

serves many mornings
8 large handfuls of organic Scottish porridge oats
2 large handfuls of ground bran
1 handful of chopped dried apricots
1 handful of chopped dried dates
1 handful of crumbled walnuts
1 handful of smashed or chopped almonds, hazelnuts or Brazil nuts

Add your porridge oats and bran to your plastic container with the apricots and dates. Add the walnuts and your other chosen nuts (I usually bash them up in a tea towel). At this point feel free to improvise, adding any other preferred dried fruits like raisins, sultanas or figs – but personally I think my combination works pretty well. This will keep for a good couple of months very happily in your airtight container, but you'll have eaten it by then, I guarantee.

making and knocking together

milk to cover
$1/2$ crunchy apple per person, washed and unpeeled

I would definitely try to make this the night or day before you want to eat it, although it can be made at the time (but you won't get the smooth silky scrumptious texture that the milk gives it overnight). I normally place double the amount of composed cereal I need (i.e. 4 portions for 2 people) into a bowl. Doubling up like this gives you enough to eat for the next couple of days. Cover with milk, grate in around $1/2$ an apple per person and stir immediately to stop the apple discolouring. Place in the fridge.

tucking in and eating

¹/₂ banana per person, peeled and sliced, or squashed
honey to taste

Remove the bowl from the fridge. You will find that it has softened and thickened, so loosen with a little milk. Add your banana, sliced or squashed. You will find that a lot of natural sweetness has come out of the dried fruit, so add honey to taste. Serve in a bowl with a dollop of yoghurt and some mixed berries.

homemade yoghurt

I love making yoghurt. For some reason it's really rewarding, I'm not sure why. I think it's the fact that it's so damn easy to turn a litre of milk into a litre of yoghurt. Things like yoghurt and bread are fantastic for kids to make, so let them have a go.

1 litre/1¾ pints full cream milk, preferably organic
1 × 500ml tub live yoghurt

Bring your milk to the boil in a thick-bottomed pan then turn the heat off. Leave for around 40 minutes until the milk has cooled down to body temperature. Use your finger to check. At this point stir or whisk in your live yoghurt. Cover and leave at room temperature for 6–8 hours, by which time you'll be amazed to see that the milk has turned into creamy yoghurt. Without getting too technical, the live culture in the yoghurt turns the natural sugar of the milk into acid. This causes the milk to thicken and taste slightly sharp. Different yoghurts may react slightly differently, i.e. some will thicken more than others, but, as a rule, all results are fantastic. Place it in the fridge to chill. It will keep for around a week.

Here are some of my favourite ways to eat yoghurt for breakfast or dessert, but don't forget it's great in marinades (see page 194) and fantastically refreshing lobbed over spicy lamb and couscous or curry and rice:

- With vanilla sugar
- With strawberries marinated in balsamic vinegar
- With mixed soft fruit
- With rosewater, honey and pistachio nuts
- With pukkolla
- With figs and a bit of brandy
- With baked fruit

tapas, munchies
and snacks

I'm a right one for munchies and snacks, and the whole tapas thing really gets me going. I must admit I love the old Boxing Day dinner so much that I do constantly try and re-enact it for the rest of the year with the snacks in this chapter. My missus, sorry, the lovely Jules, often finds me watching telly late at night after work or a band practice gnawing on some stale old bread, pickled chillies and various other preserved or recycled dinners. She always looks disgusted by my new and innovative combinations but sod it, I'm happy.

When having friends over for drinks, or if people just pop round, it's fantastic to offer them a little nibble of something. If you've got a couple of simple tricks up your sleeve they'll think you're a right little tiger and that you've made a bit of an effort for them. If you're a bit of a midnight muncher like me then check out this chapter for some finger-, bite- and snack-sized tucker.

Any combination of dishes in this chapter works extremely well but personally I like to serve them with some interesting homemade bread. Try my flat breads (pages 235–6) as they will go brilliantly with everything in this chapter.

pan-toasted almonds with a touch of chilli and sea salt

These must be the quickest thing in the world to make. Believe me, there's nothing more scrumptious with any cold drink and good company than a plate of hot, toasted, tasty almonds. Try throwing them into salads too – nothing better.

serves 8
½ tablespoon olive oil
255g/9oz shelled and peeled almonds
1–3 small dried red chillies
2 generous pinches of Maldon sea salt

Add the olive oil and almonds to a hot frying pan. Fry and kinda toast the almonds until golden brown, shaking the pan regularly to colour them evenly and accentuate their nutty flavour. Crumble in the chilli to taste and add the sea salt. Toss over and serve hot on a large plate. Bloomin' gorgeous.

tapas, munchies and snacks

smashed spiced chickpeas

This is a bastardized humous recipe, but no less tasty. I love it best smeared over thin pizza bases (see page 232) cooked on a hot griddle pan until charred, but tortillas are always a quick option.

serves 6
1 x 400g tin of chickpeas or use 170g/6oz dried ones,
    soaked and cooked until tender
a good pinch of cumin seeds, pounded
1–2 small dried red chillies, crumbled
1 clove of garlic, peeled and pounded to a paste
juice of 1 lemon
salt and freshly ground black pepper
olive oil

This is so simple to make. Really it's all about personal taste – the way I look at it is that chickpeas are really moreish but they need a good kick up the backside to really get their flavours happening. So by smashing them up and adding a good pinch of cumin for a bit of spice, a little dried chilli for a touch of heat, garlic for a bit of ooorrrgggghhh, a good squeezing of lemon juice to give it a twang and seasoning to taste, you pretty much hit the nail on the head. Then add extra virgin olive oil to loosen and flavour. Love it.

black olive tapenade

Olives with stones in are much tastier – they will make all the difference to this tapenade.

serves 6–8
250g/9oz black olives, destoned
1 clove of garlic, peeled
6 anchovy fillets
salt and freshly ground black pepper
extra virgin olive oil
juice of 1 lemon

Destone the olives by squeezing or bashing them and removing the stone. You can either very finely chop the olives, garlic and anchovies by hand or place them in a food processor and whizz until smooth. Correct the seasoning, add olive oil to loosen and, very importantly, add lemon juice to taste.

blackened sweet aubergine

Some people call this 'poor man's caviar' but I say it's 'Essex boy's caviar'.

serves 6–8
4 firm aubergines
a pinch of cumin seeds, pounded
1 clove of garlic, pounded to a paste
extra virgin olive oil
juice of 2 or 3 lemons, to taste
salt and freshly ground black pepper
1 handful of coriander, basil or parsley, chopped (optional)

Preheat the oven to its hottest setting. Place the aubergines on a tray and cook for 1 hour, until the insides are very soft. Remove from the oven, slit the skin and scrape out the insides. Add your cumin and garlic, stir in and break up. You can make this smooth or coarse, depending on how you feel. Add olive oil to loosen. Squeeze in your lemon juice and season to taste. I would never serve this hot, but it's great just warm or at room temperature. If adding herbs do this at the last minute, roughly or finely chopped.

smashed courgette paste

This is fantastic spread over toasted breads, thrown into pasta or even in ravioli with ricotta. Try to buy small firm courgettes as they have a better flavour and are not all soft and fluffy in the middle.

serves 6–8
extra virgin olive oil
2 cloves of garlic, peeled and finely chopped
1–2 small dried red chillies, crumbled
6–8 small courgettes, unevenly sliced
salt and freshly ground black pepper
1 good handful of mint, chopped
juice of 1 lemon

Put a couple of lugs of oil in a hot pan and fry your garlic and chillies for a couple of minutes. Throw in the courgettes, stir around and coat. Turn the heat down slightly and put the lid on. Give the pan a shake and stir every 5 minutes for around 35 minutes, making sure the courgettes don't catch on the bottom. Cooking with the lid on will ensure that there's a little moisture in the pan. When the courgettes are really soft, with some chunky pieces and the rest almost pulped, remove from the heat and taste carefully. Remembering that this will probably be used on bread, you may have to adjust the chilli to your taste. Season well and pour in 4 good lugs of extra virgin olive oil to flavour and loosen. Finally add your chopped mint and lemon juice.

marinated olives

The thing about olives is that there are so many varieties, so when at deli counters in supermarkets, feel free to ask to try all of them. When I've found a type I like, I buy around 500g/1lb each time. The olives can then be flavoured with fantastic things – but use dried flavourings if you want the olives to keep well.

Mix your olives in a bowl with a good sprinkling of dried oregano, a ripped-up bay leaf and some crumbled dried red chillies. Season with just pepper as olives are salty already, and add some cracked coriander seeds or fennel seeds. Then pack the olives tightly into an airtight jar and cover with a good olive oil. This is a fantastic marinade which will complement your olives, making them dead tasty and great for cooking with, using in salads or simply as finger food with drinks.

blackened marinated peppers

Fantastic as part of a tapas or antipasti selection, or serve simply with a piece of grilled fish or in salads.

serves 6
4 large peppers (2 red, 2 yellow)
1 large clove of garlic, peeled and finely sliced
1–2 small dried red chillies, crumbled
1 tablespoon coriander seeds
5 good lugs of extra virgin olive oil
a splash of red wine vinegar
salt and freshly ground black pepper
1 good handful of fresh basil

Normally I place the peppers directly on to a naked flame. This can also be done on a barbecue or under the grill. Once blackened all over, allow to steam in a covered bowl for 5 minutes. Peel and deseed. Don't wash the skins off under running water as you will lose a little of the fantastic sweetness that you've created by blackening them. I normally tear each pepper into around 8 strips and place them in a bowl. Add the garlic, chillies, coriander seeds and olive oil to the peppers with a good splash of red wine vinegar. The key is to season well to taste. Toss this and, ideally, allow to sit for an hour, tossing occasionally, before ripping in your basil and serving.

slow-cooked and stuffed baby bell chilli peppers

These are the most fantastic thing. You eat the chillies whole and they are amazing as munchies with drinks, not too hot. At the same time they make lovely flavoured olive oil which I like to add garlic and bay to for extra flavour. Great used on salads, over mozzarella and other cheeses, on pizzas and over pasta.

makes 10 portions
1kg/2lb 3oz small, round baby bell chilli peppers
a bottle of olive oil (don't panic – see below!)
1 good handful of parsley or basil
2 good handfuls of rocket
1 small handful of capers, soaked and drained
1 handful of anchovies
10 tablespoons balsamic vinegar, or enough to cover
salt and freshly ground black pepper

Halve your chillies, remove the seeds and wash in cold water. Then drain. Tightly pack into a large earthenware dish and cover with the olive oil, then place in the oven at 170°C/325°F/gas 3 for 35–45 minutes until just tender. *Carefully* remove the dish from the oven and leave to cool. Take the chillies out of the dish. Pour the fantastic flavoured olive oil back into the bottle it came from. Finely chop your parsley or basil, rocket and capers. Roughly chop the anchovies and then mix everything up in a bowl. Just before you want to serve them, dress with the balsamic vinegar, and season. Stuff this filling into your chillies and serve on a plate as tapas.

marinated anchovies

Unless you're lucky enough to get fresh ones, the best anchovies you can get hold of are nearly always salted and whole. These are still great for cooking, but to eat an anchovy like you do when abroad, draped over toasted crostini, with milky cheeses and in salads, I personally feel no matter how good the anchovy is, the salt overpowers the natural flavour of the dish. So what I do is marinate anchovies to remove their excess salt and then infuse them with other interesting flavours.

Simply take your anchovies off the bone and leave them under running water for a couple of minutes. Pat dry and place a layer snugly in a dish or on a plate. The main thing is to have something acidic to remove the salt, and a good sweet wine, lemon juice or herb vinegar will do this – add just enough to nearly cover the anchovies. Add the same amount of good olive oil and then any flavours that take your fancy, such as chilli, fennel seeds, fresh parsley, fresh thyme or flecks of garlic and lemon peel. To make all the difference, marinate in the fridge for between 2 and 16 hours before eating.

grilled butterflied sardines

serves 6–8
1 small handful of fresh breadcrumbs
a pinch of dried oregano
1–2 small dried red chillies, crumbled
1 small handful of fresh parsley, chopped
peel of 1 lemon, finely chopped
salt and freshly ground black pepper
8 large fresh sardines, scaled and gutted

Mix everything, apart from the sardines, in a bowl then remove the heads from the sardines. Open the belly of each fish. What you need to do is remove the spine and bones from the flesh. It's a bit fiddly, but well worth doing. With your left hand you need to pinch away the flesh from the spine; with your right hand pull the spine away from the flesh. You will end up with the boned fillets butterflied open. Then all you have to do is press your flavoured breadcrumb mixture on each side of the sardines.

I like to cook the fish on a very hot ridged griddle pan or barbecue. Some of the breadcrumb mix will fall off during cooking but that doesn't matter because it will have imparted its flavour by then and done its job. It literally takes 1–2 minutes to cook until crisp. Serve on a plate with some halved lemons. Fantastic. Wicked with a glass of wine.

tapas, munchies and snacks

marinated squid with chickpeas and chilli

serves 6–8

6 medium-sized squid, gutted and cleaned

1 x 400g tin of chickpeas or use 170g/6oz dried ones,
    soaked and cooked until tender

1 small finger of fresh ginger, peeled and finely sliced

around 4 lugs of extra virgin olive oil

juice of 2 lemons

2 fresh red chillies, deseeded and finely sliced

salt and freshly ground black pepper

1 handful of fresh flat-leaf parsley, finely chopped

1 handful of fresh coriander, torn

You can ask your fishmonger to clean the squid for you and score it in a criss-cross pattern. This will allow your marinade to get right in there. In a hot griddle or frying pan, or over the barbecue, sear and char the squid. It should take about a minute for the white flesh and a little longer for the tentacles. Remove and slice up the white flesh of each squid into 3 or 4 pieces, leaving the tentacles whole. Put the rest of the ingredients, except the herbs, into a bowl, then add your squid while still hot and toss everything together. Just before serving, throw in your herbs and check again for seasoning.

salted and spiced prawns

Basically what we are doing here is encrusting spicy salt on to the prawn shells.

serves 6–8

1kg/2lb 3oz small prawns, raw and whole

4 generous pinches of sea salt

6 generous pinches of mixed spices (fennel, coriander, cumin, chilli), lightly crushed

Leave the shells on the prawns, although you can remove the heads if you want. Get a wok or large pan very hot, then add the salt and spices. Toast and toss around for 30 seconds before adding your prawns. Shake vigorously and toss. Your salt and spices will stick and encrust themselves to the prawns. After a minute or two the prawns will have cooked and changed colour and should be tasty and crunchy. I normally eat the prawn shells but you don't have to.

Asian infused tuna

Try to buy firm, deep red tuna. The idea is for it to be eaten raw – just like sushi – but, in actual fact, the acidity of the lime juice starts to cook the fish.

serves 6–8
455g/1lb tuna, bluefin if possible
1 ripe avocado, peeled and diced
juice of 4–5 limes, to taste
1–2 fresh chillies, deseeded and finely chopped
3 tablespoons sesame seed oil
4 tablespoons coconut milk
1 good handful of fresh coriander, finely chopped
2 heaped tablespoons sesame seeds
a little fresh ginger, peeled and finely chopped
soy sauce, to taste

Finely dice your tuna and place in a bowl. Add the rest of the ingredients, stir and add soy sauce to season. This fantastically flavoured tuna is great on thinly sliced toasted bread.

simple salads and dressings

I love salads and, like in the last book, I've made them really simple and conversational. Try to eat salads regularly and you'll really get into them. I've spoken to so many people about what they like to eat, and you won't be surprised that most blokes when asked what they like say 'MEAT', 'MEAT AND TWO VEG' – that means chips and mash. Well, that's great – me too. But you can't beat a good salad. Even when I'm taken out to some of the most expensive restaurants in London I still always ask for the chef's mixed salad even if it's not on the menu. I think it tells you a lot about a kitchen when you order a salad – you will either get one that has been chucked together without much thought or you will get a mixture of fantastic different leaves and herbs which, when eaten, makes you think, 'God, that's nice. What was that I just ate?' A great salad can also simply be one or two things that complement each other. It doesn't have to be complicated.

So to get friendly with salads you should buy a couple of nice big salad bowls that you can put in the middle of the table, acquire some good extra virgin olive oil, some different vinegars – there's so much choice now – and buy some things that you have never thought of trying before. There's loads of new salad leaves, different types of radishes and tomatoes, etc. It's endless. Get stuck in.

mozzarella and grilled chilli salad

Another great salad that can get away with being part of an antipasti selection as well as a main course salad or sandwich filling. Simple flavours again: it's all based around the milky soft mozzarella and the slightly more refined heat of the grilled chilli. If possible try to buy buffalo mozzarella, as it's made out of buffalo milk which makes the cheese far more tasty and delicate in both texture and taste. The salad doesn't work nearly as well with that chewy horrible stuff that is used on pizzas.

I normally use 1 fresh red chilli to every ball of mozzarella, but do use more or less as you please. Prick the chillies with a knife, otherwise they can puff up and explode in your face, and place them straight on to the naked flame if you have a gas hob. If you don't have gas, put them in a pan on the highest setting of your electric hob. Both ways you need to blacken the chillies on all sides, so turn when need be. When fully blackened, place in a sandwich bag, wrap in clingfilm or cover in a bowl for 5 minutes until cool. This will steam the skins and make peeling and deseeding easier.

While the chillies are steaming, gently rip up your mozzarella into 4 or 5 pieces and randomly place on a large plate. Peel and deseed the chillies and slice lengthways as thinly as you like. It's quite important to scatter them evenly over the mozzarella and very important to wash your hands after doing so before you rub your eyes or anything else! Now rip up some purple and green basil over the top, and sprinkle with sea salt and freshly ground black pepper. Add a little squeeze of lemon juice and a generous lug of olive oil. Nice one.

squashed cherry tomato and smashed olive salad

This is probably the quickest salad I make, but no less tasty for that. Very few ingredients, simple flavours, complete sense. Try to make use of the wider range of cherry tomatoes available now: yellow, tiger and plum cherry tomatoes for instance. And, as I always say, it's much better, tastewise, to buy olives with their stones still in than without. Trust me.

Always going along the line of 4 parts tomatoes to 1 part olives, simply squash your tomatoes into a bowl. I always have to put one hand over the tomatoes as I do this as juice and pips go everywhere – generally on me. You can be as rough with the tomatoes as you like as the salad looks much better rough and rustic than perfect and pretty. Then gently smash the olives on a board with a hard object – a cup or a rolling-pin. Remove the stones, throw the olives in with the tomatoes and toss together.

That's the basis of the salad made now, but what you've done already makes complete sense in cooking. Tomatoes need salt, olives are preserved in salt, you've squeezed the juice out of the tomatoes which in return draws the salt and the smoky flavour out of the olives. This makes the olives very edible and the tomatoes damn tasty. That's the most important bit done; all we can do now is enhance it. This can be done to your personal taste with a couple of dribbles of vinegar, preferably red wine or herb, some freshly ground black pepper and 2 or 3 good lugs of olive oil. And just before serving, rip in as much basil as you can afford and even a handful of rocket if you have some. Lovely.

PS If you have any leftovers then toss them in with some hot spaghetti.

couscous with grilled summer vegetables and loadsa herbs

This couscous recipe is quite a bit different from the norm because instead of boiling or steaming the couscous you just feed it from raw with a really tasty dressing. This means it keeps a slight bite which I think is more interesting for a salad.

serves 4
255g/9oz couscous
285ml/¹/₂ pint cold water
3 red peppers
1 handful of asparagus, trimmed and peeled if need be
2 or 3 small firm courgettes/patty pans, sliced
1 small bunch of spring onions, trimmed and finely sliced
2–4 fresh red chillies, deseeded and finely sliced
3 good handfuls of mixed fresh herbs (basil, coriander,
    mint, flat-leaf parsley)
2 × olive oil and lemon juice dressing (page 81)
salt and freshly ground black pepper
red wine vinegar

Place the couscous in a bowl with the cold water. This will start to soften the couscous and you will see the water disappear as it soaks in. While the couscous is softening, we need to blacken the peppers. I do this by placing the peppers directly on to the naked flame of my gas hob. If you don't have gas, then blacken under the grill. Both ways you need to blacken the peppers on all sides, so turn when need be. When fully blackened, place in a sandwich bag, wrap in clingfilm or cover in a bowl for 5 minutes until cool. This will steam the skins and make peeling and deseeding easier. Remove the skins and seeds and roughly chop.

On a very hot ridged grill pan, lightly char the asparagus and courgettes or patty pans on both sides then toss them into the bowl of couscous with the peppers, spring onions, chillies and ripped-up herbs. Mix well. Add the olive oil and lemon juice dressing and toss well. Finally, taste and season with salt and pepper and a couple of dribbles of red wine vinegar for a slight twang. It's a beautiful thing.

warm salad of winter leaves, bacon and Jerusalem artichokes

As far as salads go, this is a real hearty one, full of flavour and pretty damn gutsy. The idea behind warm salads is that you have interesting and slightly more robust salad leaves, usually mixed with sautéed vegetables or roasted meat. Anything from chicken livers, smoky bacon and scallops to roasted tomatoes, pine nuts and caramelized onions, anything really. Smoky bacon and Jerusalem artichokes is a brilliant combination.

Jerusalem artichokes are becoming more common in supermarkets now, but don't confuse them with globe artichokes, which look like big fat thistles. Jerusalem artichokes look more like new potatoes gone mad. For this recipe I normally use around 2 artichokes and 2 strips of bacon per person, but it really is up to you. I also use any combination of radicchio, cos, oak leaf, curly endive, rocket and baby spinach.

Rip the leaves up and place in a salad bowl or on a plate. I prefer to scrub the Jerusalem artichokes instead of peeling them, before cooking in salted boiling water until just soft. Cool under cold running water, drain, and slice as you would sautéed potatoes. Then in a large frying pan fry some dry-cured streaky bacon, which should be sliced across as thick as you like. When golden crisp, remove from the pan and put to one side. Add your sliced artichoke to the pan with a small lug of oil, a little butter and some salt and freshly ground black pepper. Shake the pan occasionally, adding the bacon back into the pan when the artichokes are also golden and crisp. Sprinkle over the salad leaves and drizzle generously with either the basil and balsamic vinegar dressing (page 80) or the mustard and herb vinegar dressing (page 81).

watercress, rocket, sweet pear, walnut and Parmesan salad

What a pukka combination, simple and classy. Don't try to make
this when you feel like it, make it when you can buy perfect pears
otherwise it will taste naff. For one person I normally use
around half a pear, 2 big handfuls of watercress and 2 big
handfuls of rocket. If the pear skins are nice I just give them
a wash, if not I remove them with a peeler. Then cut them
in half and deseed. It doesn't really matter how you cut

them up. Sometimes in big rough chunks, maybe sliced up or even grated. Then place into
a bowl with the watercress and rocket. The pepperiness of the leaves works so well with the
sweetness of the pear. Drizzle with good extra virgin olive oil just to coat, a small squeeze
of lemon juice (because the pear juice is slightly acidic but very tasty), and season
well with salt and freshly ground black pepper. Toss all this together and serve.
Shave over some Parmesan or pecorino, crumble your nuts over and tuck in.
I love this salad with roasted meat or as a starter on its own.

crunchy Thai salad

The thing I love about this salad is that it's so crunchy and tasty and you just know that it's really really good for you. Any combination of the following ingredients is great: beansprouts, finely sliced green and red peppers, baby spinach, finely sliced and deseeded red or green chillies, rocket, sliced spring onions, peeled, gutted and sliced cucumbers, finely sliced Chinese or Savoy cabbage, whole sugar snap peas and herbs like mint, basil and coriander. Dress with the Thai dressing on page 80. Then sprinkle with some lightly toasted cashew nuts or sesame seeds. Fantastic. If you want to make this more substantial then toss in some cooked and chilled egg noodles.

mixed leaf salad with mozzarella, mint, peach and prosciutto

Try to get hold of buffalo mozzarella. I like to crumble a little bit of dried chilli over my mozzarella, but I'm a chilli freak and you may not be, so you don't have to! And use any mixed leaves you fancy.

If I make this for my lunch I'll use one nice, ripe peach, a ball of mozzarella and a couple of slices of prosciutto. Pinch the skin and peel from the bottom to the top then quarter them. Rip the mozzarella into small pieces and place on a plate with the peaches. Lightly season. Lay a couple of slices of prosciutto over the top. Dress your mixed salad leaves and torn-up mint with a little of the olive oil and lemon juice dressing (page 81). Throw the leaves on top of the plate.

salad of boiled potatoes, avocado and cress

I had to do this salad, even though cress must be one of the tackiest things in the world. For some reason I'm absolutely addicted to it and love it to bits. This is my favourite combination.

serves 4–6
1 large ripe avocado
700g/1½lb scrubbed new potatoes
3 packs of cress, washed
olive oil
juice of 1–2 lemons
salt and freshly ground black pepper

Cook the new potatoes in salted boiling water until very tender, then drain. Slice the avocado in half and remove the stone. Peel and slice it lengthways into thick slices or chunks (however you like really) and place in a bowl. Slice any large potatoes in half – this will expose their flesh to the olive oil and lemon juice. If they are small, leave them whole. Add to the bowl. Throw the cress in, then add a couple of good lugs of olive oil and lemon juice to taste. Season and toss over. Serve on a big plate, scattered with any remaining cress. This is brilliant with chicken, fish or as a salad on its own, especially in the summer.

salad of marinated charred squid with cannellini beans, rocket and chilli

serves 4–6

1kg/2lb 3oz squid, trimmed and gutted

salt and freshly ground black pepper

1 400g tin of cannellini beans, or use 170g/6oz dried ones,
    soaked and cooked until tender

1–2 fresh chillies, red and green

2 good handfuls of rocket

juice of 2 limes or 1 lemon

olive oil

extra virgin olive oil

Try to get your fishmonger to skin and gut your squid for you. Score the squid lightly in a casual criss-cross fashion. Set it to one side while you get a griddle pan very very hot. You can also use a wok or the barbecue. Season the squid lightly just before cooking, then add it to the pan. After a minute it should be nicely charred, so turn it over and cook for a further minute then remove it and put it aside. Heat up the cannellini beans and sprinkle them into a bowl. Add the sliced chillies to the bowl with the rocket, lime or lemon juice and olive oil, and season. Cut the squid at irregular angles and toss it in with the rest of the ingredients. A good drizzle of extra virgin olive oil over the top will finish it off nicely.

celery, celeriac, parsley and pomegranate salad

This is a really clean salad, fantastic with fish or cold meats. For it to be as delicate as it should be, the celery and celeriac should be very finely sliced. You can do this by hand with a knife or with a mandolin slicer, which you can pick up really cheaply. It will make the job so much easier. I normally use 1 whole celeriac to 1 head of celery.

All you have to do is strip back the celery and peel the celeriac and then finely slice. Place in a bowl with some chopped flat-leaf parsley and a handful of pomegranate seeds (make sure you use just the red seeds, not the bitter yellow stuff). Season and dress with olive oil and lemon juice dressing (page 81). This salad can be dressed a little before you need it, as opposed to at the table. Place on a large plate and sprinkle with some extra pomegranate seeds. Sometimes I crumble goat's cheese over this, or some ricotta which I encrust with dried herbs, salt and pepper, drizzled with olive oil and baked until golden in a hot oven.

dressings

Talk about simple things making me happy. Why is it a twenty-four-year-old boy thinks he's really clever just by making his dressings in a jam jar? I feel like a bit of a trainspotter really. It sounds almost too simple but, the fact is, we all end up with empty jam jars. Just chuck all your dressing ingredients into a jam jar, tighten the lid and shake up. Dress your salad, and any leftovers can remain in the jar, in the back of the fridge, raring to dress your next salad. And the best thing is that there's no washing up of bowls, whisks and bottles, just a jam jar.

I've found that the vinegar-based dressings will taste great for a week or so, but the dressings with lemon or lime juice or dairy products in them will only taste good for a couple of days. On pages 80–81 you will find 6 tasty and simple dressings. Each will make enough to dress a salad for 4 people, but feel free to double the amounts if you need more.

basil, balsamic vinegar and pine nut dressing

2 tablespoons balsamic vinegar
5 tablespoons extra virgin olive oil
1 good handful of chopped fresh basil
1 good handful of pine nuts, toasted and chopped
salt and freshly ground black pepper, to taste

coriander and crème fraîche dressing

3 tablespoons extra virgin olive oil
3 tablespoons crème fraîche
3 teaspoons Dijon mustard
2–3 tablespoons lemon juice
2 handfuls of fresh coriander, pounded or finely chopped
salt and freshly ground black pepper, to taste

Thai dressing

4 tablespoons fresh lime juice
3 tablespoons olive oil
1 tablespoon sesame seed oil
1 tablespoon soy sauce
a good pinch of brown sugar
1 tablespoon fresh ginger, peeled and finely chopped
$\frac{1}{2}$ clove of garlic, finely sliced
1 fresh red chilli, deseeded and finely sliced
1 large handful of fresh coriander and basil, chopped

mustard and herb vinegar dressing

6 tablespoons olive oil

2 tablespoons Dijon mustard

2 tablespoons red or white herb vinegar

1 level teaspoon salt

1 teaspoon freshly ground black pepper

olive oil and lemon juice dressing

2 tablespoons lemon juice

5 tablespoons olive oil

salt and freshly ground black pepper, to taste

sweet cherry tomato dressing

1 teacup of ripe, washed cherry tomatoes, finely chopped

$1/2$ clove of garlic, finely sliced

6 tablespoons olive oil

2 tablespoons red wine vinegar

1 handful of basil, pounded or finely chopped

a pinch of dried chilli

salt and freshly ground black pepper, to taste

2 anchovy fillets, chopped (optional)

soups and broths

Good soups are fantastic comfort food. They're dead simple to make, but the most important thing to remember is that you must use good stock. Now before you start thinking you're going to have to be boiling things for hours, let me tell you what stock is to me at home. It's Sunday night, we've had roast chicken for dinner with all the trimmings and now I'm washing up. Two things can happen: one, I can pick up the remains of the chicken and chuck them in the bin; or two, I can throw the remains into a pot with some root veg (carrots, onions, celery and some sprigs of herbs from the window-box), cover with water, then bring to the boil and simmer for an hour. There you go, fantastic tasty simple stock. I usually strain it before putting it in containers and freezing it, where it just sits waiting to be used for sauces, gravy or soups. Easy peasy. Not a stock cube in sight. If you're vegetarian then great stocks can still be made with lots of fresh vegetables – most importantly, use a handful of dried mushrooms as these will give the stock a really substantial flavour. You'll find 3 stock recipes on pages 275–6.

potato and Jerusalem artichoke soup with thyme, mascarpone and hazelnuts

serves 4–6

2 knobs of butter

2 cloves of garlic, finely chopped

1 onion, finely chopped

455g/1lb Jerusalem artichokes, peeled and chopped

225g/8oz potatoes, peeled and chopped

1 good handful of thyme leaves, picked

1.1 litre/2 pints chicken or vegetable stock (pages 275–6)

155g/5½oz mascarpone cheese

salt and freshly ground black pepper

around 200g/7oz hazelnuts, toasted and broken up

In a large pan, melt the butter and slowly fry the garlic, onion, artichokes, potatoes and thyme. Add the stock, then bring to the boil and simmer for about 30 minutes until the potatoes and artichokes are tender. Liquidize chunky or to a purée. Reheat, adding the mascarpone and correcting the seasoning. Serve sprinkled with the hazelnuts.

Mary's Saturday soup and dumplings

Mary is the mother of my mate Kevin and her Saturday soup is famous in east London. It's great comfort food that originates from the West Indies. There are tales behind its name but basically it's a chunky, robust soup that is supposed to use up any leftover vegetables. Who cares where its name comes from — it's bloody tasty, even on a Monday, and that's all that matters! I've changed Mary's recipe to suit my taste — I'll probably get a slap for it, but that's cooking and you can do what you like!

serves 6–8

dumplings
4 heaped tablespoons self-raising flour
4 heaped tablespoons cornmeal
   (if unavailable use plain flour)
55g/2oz or ¼ pack of soft butter
salt and freshly ground black pepper
water to bind

soup
680g/1½lb stewing lamb or beef, diced
salt and freshly ground black pepper
olive oil
1 medium onion, finely sliced
1 medium carrot, roughly chopped

2 tablespoons coriander seeds
2 handfuls of fresh thyme
2 large sweet potatoes, peeled and
   chopped into chunks
1 butternut squash (or 455g/1lb pumpkin),
   peeled, deseeded and chopped into
   chunks
455g/1lb white yam, peeled and chopped
   into chunks
1.1 litres/2 pints chicken stock (page 275)
1 × 400ml tin of coconut milk
255g/9oz okra
2–3 fresh red chillies, deseeded
   and chopped

Rub together the flour, cornmeal, butter and seasoning, adding water bit by bit to form a stiff dough. Roll into balls slightly smaller than golf balls and put to one side.

In a large pot, fry the seasoned meat in a little olive oil until lightly coloured. Add the onion, carrot, coriander seeds and thyme. Shake around and soften slightly before adding the sweet potatoes, squash and yam. Turn down the heat and cook for 20 minutes with the lid on, shaking regularly. Stir in the stock, lay the dumplings on top and simmer for 40 minutes with the lid on before adding the coconut milk and okra and cooking for a final 10 minutes. Carefully season, tasting as you go. Sprinkle with the chillies before serving. Scrummy.

PS Instead of throwing away the squash seeds, roast them in a little oil and salt until crisp. Serve either sprinkled over the soup or on their own with drinks.

squash, Parma ham hock, sage, onion and barley broth

In Italy, when slicing Parma and prosciutto ham, the first half, which is really lean, is used in salads and meat plates. The next bit of the ham is fatty and more sinewy, lending itself to being wrapped around fish and meat and roasting. What's left of the ham is the hock, and this is great cooked slowly with beans or used in soups. In England we don't seem to cook much with hocks and I've found that in supermarkets they are either binned or left to one side. So ask at the deli counter if you can have one. You should pay half the price for the hock compared to the lean ham. If not, have a word with the manager. If you find you can't get hold of one then a gammon or bacon hock will work just as well.

serves 4–6
1 red onion, finely chopped
1 tablespoon coriander seeds, crushed
2 cloves of garlic, peeled and finely chopped
olive oil
1 butternut squash, peeled, deseeded and roughly chopped
2 good handfuls of fresh sage
1 good handful of pearl barley
1.1 litres/2 pints chicken or vegetable stock (pages 275–6)
about 680g/1½lb Parma ham hock, skin removed
sea salt and freshly ground black pepper
extra virgin olive oil

optional
1 handful of chestnuts, shelled
a pinch of dried chilli and a pinch of nutmeg

In a large pot slowly fry the onion, coriander seeds and garlic in a little olive oil until softened. Then add the squash, sage, chestnuts if you're using them and pearl barley. Stir in the stock and add your Parma ham hock. Bring to the boil then simmer for 1½ hours. Remove the hock, discard the bone if there is one, then break the meat up into small pieces with two forks and leave to one side. Take half the soup and liquidize it to make it smooth. Add it back to the pan with your broken-up ham, then season carefully with sea salt and freshly ground black pepper. Add a bit of chilli and ground nutmeg if you like, to taste. Feel free to loosen with a little extra stock if need be. Serve in a bowl with a little peppery extra virgin olive oil and some hot crusty bread.

seafood broth, ripped herbs, toasted bread and garlic aïoli

This broth is such a cracker. If a friend served this to me I'd be well impressed. Try it – you'll love it. I base it around mussels because they're tasty and damn good value. You can add any other seafood you like. The aïoli is not essential with this, but it is fantastic and you should give it a go.

serves 6
795g/1¾lb mixed seafood (squid, red mullet, prawns and monkfish)
795g/1¾lb mussels
1 × 400g tin or 8 large ripe plum tomatoes
extra virgin olive oil
2 cloves of garlic, peeled and sliced
2–3 fresh red chillies, deseeded and sliced
2 good handfuls of courgettes, finely sliced
2 large glasses of white wine
salt and freshly ground black pepper
2 good handfuls of mixed fresh herbs, ripped
   (basil, parsley, fennel, marjoram)
garlic aïoli (page 276)
1 lemon

First clean up your seafood. I normally get my fishmonger to scale, gut and fillet the fish and clean the squid for me – it saves making a mess. Then all I have to do is pull the beards off the mussels. If using fresh tomatoes, remove their cores and place in boiling water for 1 minute – this will loosen their skins – then rinse quickly under cold water and remove the skins.

Into a very hot pan swiftly pour 4 good lugs of extra virgin olive oil and add the mussels. Flick the garlic, chillies and courgettes on top, shake the pan around, then add the white wine. While this is sizzling away, really squash in the tomatoes and lay your mixed seafood on top. Turn the heat right down and simmer for around 5 minutes until all the shellfish are open. Discard any that remain closed. Season with salt and freshly ground black pepper and add your herbs. Serve the broth in big bowls over some toasted bread and, if you want to make it really pukka, add a big lob of garlic aïoli on top and a wedge of lemon.

fragrant Thai broth

This is a really satisfying and almost cleansing soup. It's easy to vary this broth by using different seafood or herbs and even by adding noodles to make it more substantial. It's quite classic to have finely sliced fried onions sprinkled on top just before serving – nice idea, but another pan to wash up!

serves 4

3 sticks of lemon grass, crushed and bruised
2 fingers of ginger, peeled, crushed and bruised
6 kaffir lime leaves, ripped up
1.1 litres/2 pints chicken stock (page 275)
1–2 heaped tablespoons sugar
around 4–6 tablespoons fish sauce, to taste
juice of 1–2 limes
2 or 3 large prawns per person, shelled, deveined and butterflied
1 good handful of fresh coriander and basil

garnish

2 fresh chillies, sliced
1 red pepper, finely sliced
4 spring onions, finely sliced

In a pestle and mortar bash together the lemon grass, ginger and lime leaves. Place in a pot with the stock, bring to the boil, then simmer for 10 minutes. Taste – it should be tasty and fragrant, but slightly bland. So add the sugar, fish sauce and lime juice to taste. What you are trying to achieve with these 3 ingredients is a slightly sweet, sour, salty and savoury balance – but, to be honest, this is a personal thing, so add them bit by bit and keep tasting until you have a flavour you're happy with.

Now add the prawns to the broth and cook for 1 minute. Remove the prawns and divide them between 4 bowls, topped with the fresh herbs and garnish. You can now finish the soup by pouring your broth into each bowl. I like a bit of drama so I pour the broth into my glass Bodum teapot, plunging the fresh herbs into it. Visually this looks great but infusing the perfume from the herbs at the last minute like this also gives you a fresh and vibrant flavour. Feel free to improvise on the herbs – you don't have to stick to coriander and basil.

pasta and risotto

gennaro

If you can crack one of these two then your mates are gonna think you're a bit clever. A good pasta dish or a good risotto just can't be beaten. We're not talking about flashy food, we're talking about something really tasty, something mouth-watering and something with a real personal touch just waiting to be eaten – that's what it's all about, whether you're in a restaurant, sitting down with your family or having a dinner party. Give 'em a try.

In this chapter you'll find amazingly quick dried pasta recipes, as well as some gutsy homemade fresh pasta for all occasions and seasons. The basic risotto recipe is fantastic, giving you the perfect creamy base with some extremely simple variations – try them all and make up some of your own too.

fresh pasta

Being able to make good fresh pasta is in my eyes one of the best things I've ever learnt in cooking. It allows you to put character into the pasta as well as into the sauce, making snacks, lunches, dinners and dinner parties damn handsome and wholesome. And people can tell it's homemade and just love it. You've got to try it – it will be a real asset to your repertoire. The basic pasta recipe on the next page can be made in a mixer or food processor but I prefer doing it by hand so I can feel what's happening as I work the dough. Remember: save the egg whites that you're not using to make batters and meringues.

blinding pasta recipe

serves 4
250g/9oz strong flour
250g/9oz semolina flour (if unavailable, strong flour will do)
3 large free-range eggs
8 egg yolks

Place both flours on a clean surface. Make a well in the centre and add the eggs and yolks. With a fork break up the eggs as you bring in the flour. Stir with the fork until you have a dough which you can work with your hands. Knead well until you have a smooth, silky and elastic dough and a clean surface. Wrap the dough in clingfilm and rest it in the fridge for a while.

I use a pasta machine to roll out my pasta into thin sheets about 10cm/4inches wide. Try to get one – they're great. They rarely break and only set you back about £25. However, you can use a rolling-pin – it just takes a little longer to get the pasta as thin. Divide your ball of pasta into 4 pieces and keep covered. Working with one ball at a time, flatten out with your hand and run through the thickest setting on your machine. Fold in half and repeat this process several times, to give you perfect, textured pasta. Dust the sheet of pasta on both sides with flour before running it through the settings – I usually repeat this 4 or 5 times, dusting and moving the setting in each time until I have the desired thickness (normally about 1–2mm thick, depending on the type of pasta I am making). It does take practice, but once you've cracked it, you'll be knocking up pasta like no one's business. It's all about getting to grips with how pasta works. It will stay fresh in the fridge for half a day or it can be dried (see page 101) and stored in airtight containers.

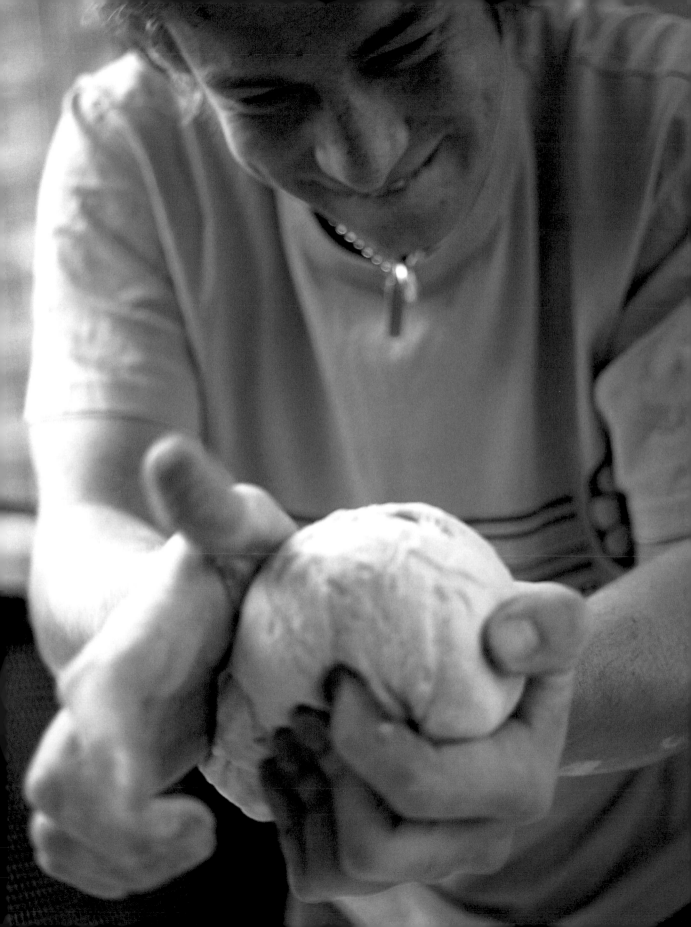

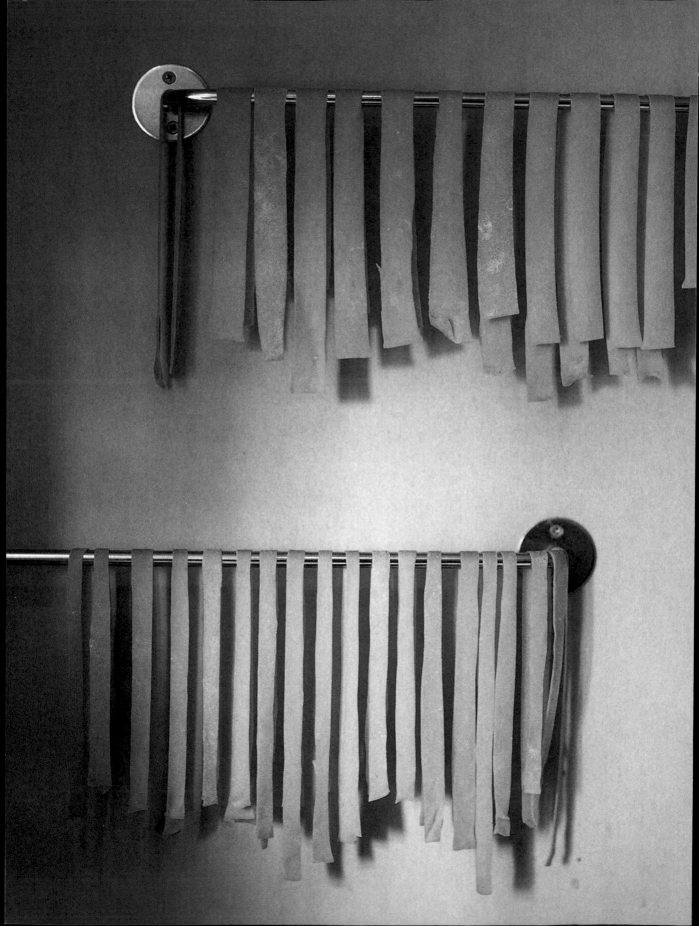

shaping pasta from a sheet

So you've got your pasta sheets in front of you – now all you have to do is shape them. Check out the recipes on pages 103–23 using stracci, pappardelle, tagliatelle, ravioli and tortellini. There are so many things you can make by simply cutting, folding or filling pasta, so what are you waiting for? Get cracking.

drying pasta

I generally make fresh pasta at home on special occasions or when friends are coming round. Saying that, I always tend to double or triple the recipe, making much more than I need, and I dry the rest, cutting it into any shape or size – this is great because it means I then have a supply of homemade pasta to last me, normally, a couple of weeks until the next time I make pasta. Superb.

To dry it, all you need to do is place the pasta on a rack or hang it on a coathanger or something similar for 1 or 2 days until completely dry. To test, scrunch a piece in your hand and it should crumble and snap into small brittle pieces quite easily. Dried pasta can be stored in airtight containers for a good couple of months once dried properly.

stracci

Stracci basically means 'scratched', and I love it because you can slice and scratch the sheets of pasta as you like. Cut your pieces into varied shapes and sizes with different angles and lengths (see picture on page 104). Go for interesting shapes.

stracci, spicy aubergines, tomatoes, basil and Parmesan

serves 4

1 large aubergine, cut into 1cm/$\frac{1}{2}$ inch dice

1 teaspoon coriander seeds, cracked

1–2 dried red chillies, crumbled

olive oil

1 × 400g tin of good Italian peeled plum tomatoes,
    drained and chopped

2 handfuls of black olives, destoned

salt and freshly ground black pepper

a splash of red wine vinegar (optional)

fresh stracci: 1 × pasta recipe (page 98)

2 handfuls of fresh basil

2 handfuls of grated Parmesan cheese

In a large hot pan, fry the aubergine, coriander seeds and chillies in a couple of generous lugs of olive oil until they are nice and golden. Add more olive oil if needed. Add the chopped tomatoes and cook for 5 minutes before adding the olives. Continue cooking until you have a lovely 'saucey' consistency. Season to taste at this point with salt, pepper and maybe a splash of red wine vinegar. Cook the stracci in salted boiling water until al dente. Drain and throw into the sauce. Toss over, rip in the basil and serve with grated Parmesan on top.

stracci with Gorgonzola, mascarpone, marjoram and walnuts

serves 4
1 clove of garlic, peeled and finely chopped
olive oil
2 good handfuls of marjoram, washed and picked
140g/5oz Gorgonzola cheese
255g/9oz mascarpone cheese
fresh stracci: 1 x pasta recipe (page 98)
around 200g/7oz walnuts, shells removed
salt and freshly ground black pepper
1 good handful of grated Parmesan cheese

In a pan fry the garlic in a little olive oil with the marjoram until softened. Turn down the heat and add the Gorgonzola and mascarpone. Slowly melt the cheeses in – don't let them boil. Cook your stracci in salted boiling water until al dente. Now turn up the heat under the cheese – again, don't let this boil – throwing in half the walnuts. Season to taste. Toss the drained stracci into the sauce, coat and serve sprinkled with the rest of the walnuts and the Parmesan.

pappardelle

Cut the sheets of pasta to about the length of a shoebox. Fold them over twice, making sure you have dusted them generously on both sides with flour. Now cut into slices approximately 4cm/1½ inches wide (see picture on page 107) and you have your pappardelle. Remember to gently toss and jiggle the pappardelle around to separate the lengths of pasta once you have cut them. This will remove any excess flour.

pappardelle with rabbit, herbs and cream

serves 4
2 good handfuls of fresh thyme, leaves picked
salt and freshly ground black pepper
olive oil
rind of 2 lemons, peeled
4 legs of rabbit
1 clove of garlic, peeled and finely chopped
1 small red onion, peeled and finely chopped
3 good glasses of white wine
1 × 285ml carton of double cream
fresh pappardelle: 1 × pasta recipe (page 98)
1 good handful of grated Parmesan cheese

Smash your thyme with a little pinch of salt in a pestle and mortar and scrunch together with a couple of lugs of olive oil and the lemon rind. Massage this on to the legs of rabbit and set aside for 15 minutes to 1 hour. In a hot pan that you can put a tight-fitting lid on to later, fry the rabbit until lightly golden. Then add the marinade, garlic and onion and continue cooking until slightly softened. Add the white wine, place on the lid and simmer very slowly for about 1 hour until tender. Continue checking to make sure that the liquid in the pan does not dry up (adding a little water if necessary). When the rabbit is cooked, allow to cool slightly then use 2 forks to remove all the meat from the bones. Put the meat back into the pan with the cooking juices, add the cream and reheat. Cook your pappardelle in salted boiling water until al dente. Drain the pasta and toss with the creamy meat sauce. Remove from the heat, correct the seasoning and add the Parmesan, toss again and serve.

pappardelle, spicy sausage meat and mixed wild mushrooms

You don't have to use your own freshly-made pasta for this – you can get some really nice curly dried stuff, like the pasta seen here which I nicked from my mate Gennaro.

serves 4
1 onion, peeled and finely chopped
1 clove of garlic, peeled and finely chopped
255g/9oz of the best spicy sausages you can find, meat removed from skin
olive oil
2 good handfuls of fresh thyme, leaves picked
1–2 small dried red chillies, crumbled, to taste
400g/14oz mixed wild mushrooms (girolles, chanterelles, ceps or blewits,
    oyster and shiitake), torn
fresh pappardelle: 1 × pasta recipe (page 98)
salt and freshly ground black pepper
3 good knobs of butter
1 handful of parsley, chopped
1 handful of grated Parmesan cheese

Fry the onion, garlic and sausage meat in a little olive oil until lightly golden. Add the thyme, chillies and mushrooms. Continue to fry, cooking away any moisture from the mushrooms. Cook the pappardelle in salted boiling water until al dente. Reserve a little cooking water. Remove the mushrooms from the heat, season to taste and loosen with 3 knobs of butter and a little cooking water from the pasta. Toss the drained pasta with the mushrooms and serve sprinkled with lots of parsley and some grated Parmesan.

tagliatelle

Cut the sheets of pasta to about the length of a shoebox. Fold them over twice, making sure you have dusted them generously on both sides with flour. Now cut into slices around 1cm/½ inch wide (see picture on page 110) and you have your tagliatelle. Remember to gently toss and jiggle the tagliatelle around to separate the lengths of pasta once you have cut them. This will remove any excess flour.

tagliatelle with saffron, seafood and cream

serves 4
a good pinch of saffron
1 glass of white wine
fresh tagliatelle: 1 × pasta recipe (page 98)
olive oil
1 large clove of garlic, finely chopped
680g/1½lb mixed seafood (red mullet, scallops,
   clams, debearded mussels, prawns, squid)
1 × 285ml carton of double cream
salt and freshly ground black pepper
fennel tops, parsley or dill to garnish, chopped

Soak the saffron in the white wine. Cook the tagliatelle in salted boiling water until al dente. Add a little oil and the garlic to a frying pan and cook until softened. Add the clams and mussels, shake the pan around and add the white wine and saffron mixture. Bring to the boil, and discard any shellfish that remain closed. Then add the rest of the seafood and the cream. Simmer for 3–4 minutes, season to taste, add the drained tagliatelle and serve scattered with a few chopped fennel tops, parsley or dill.

tagliatelle with tomato sauce, spinach and crumbled ricotta

serves 4

1 large clove of garlic, chopped
a pinch of dried chilli
olive oil
2 × 400g tins of whole plum tomatoes
red wine vinegar, to taste
salt and freshly ground black pepper
fresh tagliatelle: 1 × pasta recipe (page 98)
255g/9oz fresh spinach, washed
255g/9oz fresh ricotta (preferably buffalo), seasoned and crumbled
extra virgin olive oil

Fry the garlic and dried chilli in a little olive oil until softened. Add the tomatoes, bring to the boil, then reduce the heat to a simmer. The tomatoes should remain whole until they have cooked down into a thickish sauce. Break them up with a fork or spoon. Remove from the heat and season carefully to taste with a little red wine vinegar, salt, freshly ground black pepper and some good olive oil.

Cook the tagliatelle in salted boiling water until al dente. At the same time steam the spinach in a colander above the pasta. Drain the tagliatelle and stir into the tomato sauce. Serve with a generous amount of spinach on top and scattered with the ricotta. Finish with a drizzle of peppery extra virgin olive oil.

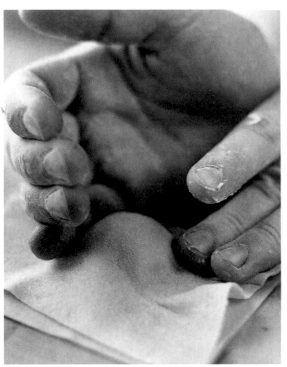

making ravioli

After rolling out the pasta sheets to about 1mm thick and 10cm/4inches wide (see page 104) you can fill them with your chosen filling to make ravioli. Work with 1 sheet at a time, covering the rest with a damp cloth.

Stage 1

Lay your pasta sheet on a generously flour-dusted surface with a good heaped teaspoon of filling in the middle of the sheet at one end. Repeat this all the way along the pasta at 5cm/2inch intervals. Using a clean pastry brush dipped in a little water, lightly, evenly and thoroughly brush the pasta around the piles of filling. This will stick the pasta together. Place a second, similar-sized sheet of pasta on top of the first.

Stage 2

Working from one end of the pasta to the other, push the sheets together and around each mound of filling. Do this gently with the base of your palm, cupping and enclosing each filling in the pasta making sure you extract all the air.

Stage 3

Now cut the ravioli to shape with a knife or crinkly cutter.

Stage 4

You can cook them straight away or keep them in the fridge on a flour-dusted tray for 3–4 hours if you want to eat them later.

ravioli of minted asparagus with potatoes and mascarpone

serves 4–6

225g/8oz potatoes, peeled

680g/1½lb asparagus, bases trimmed and stalks peeled
  (if need be)

1 clove of garlic, finely chopped

olive oil

salt and freshly ground black pepper

1 good handful of fresh mint, leaves picked and chopped

1 × fresh pasta recipe (page 98)

2 large knobs of butter (or ¼ pack)

2 heaped tablespoons mascarpone cheese, lightly seasoned

1 handful of grated Parmesan cheese

Cook the potatoes in salted boiling water until tender and drain. Remove the tips of the asparagus and set to one side. Finely slice the stalks and fry with the garlic in a little olive oil until tender, placing a lid on the pan. Remove from the heat, add the potato and mash together. Season carefully and add half the chopped mint to taste. Fill your ravioli with a heaped teaspoon of filling (page 113) and cook in salted boiling water with the asparagus tips for 3–4 minutes. Drain and toss the ravioli and asparagus tips with the butter, mascarpone, Parmesan and the rest of the mint.

ravioli of creamed ricotta, toasted pine nuts, Parmesan and loadsa herbs

serves 4–6

400g/14oz ricotta cheese

1 egg yolk

2 good handfuls of grated Parmesan cheese

2 handfuls of pine nuts, toasted and crushed

3 large handfuls of mixed herbs (green and purple basil, parsley),
   roughly chopped

salt and freshly ground black pepper

a pinch of nutmeg

1 × fresh pasta recipe (page 98)

extra virgin olive oil

With a fork, beat the ricotta, egg yolk and most of the Parmesan together until light and creamy. Stir in your pine nuts and herbs and season carefully with salt, pepper and nutmeg. Fill your ravioli with a good teaspoon of filling (page 113) and cook in salted boiling water for 3–4 minutes. Serve drizzled with extra virgin olive oil and the remaining Parmesan.

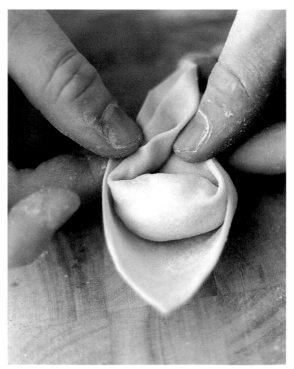

making tortellini

After rolling out the pasta sheets to about 1mm thick and 10cm/4inches wide (see page 98) you can fill them with your chosen filling to make tortellini. Work with 1 sheet at a time, covering the rest with a damp cloth.

Stage 1

Lay a sheet of pasta out on a flour-dusted surface. Cut into 10 x 10cm/4 × 4inch squares. On each square, place a good teaspoon of filling just off-centre. With a clean pastry brush evenly brush a little water around each mound of filling. Do this thoroughly to guarantee a good seal.

Stage 2

Fold each square in half from corner to corner, enclosing the filling – don't worry if they look a bit uneven as we want them to look homemade. Tightly seal the tortellini together by cupping your hand around each mound of filling and pressing down. Make sure all the air is extracted.

Stage 3

With the flat edge of each tortellini facing you, roll them once towards the tip.

Stage 4

Bring the two side flaps into the centre and squeeze them together tightly where they meet. You can cook them straight away or keep them in the fridge on a flour-dusted tray for 3–4 hours if you want to eat them later.

tortellini of ricotta, lemon, Parmesan and sage butter

serves 4–6
400g/14oz ricotta cheese, preferably buffalo
juice and zest of 2 lemons
1 good handful of grated pecorino cheese
1 good handful of grated Parmesan cheese
salt and freshly ground black pepper
1 × fresh pasta recipe (page 98)
2 good knobs of butter
1 good handful of sage, leaves picked

With a fork mix together the ricotta, lemon zest, pecorino and most of the Parmesan, and season carefully. Fill your tortellini with a teaspoon of filling (page 113) and cook in salted boiling water for 3–4 minutes. Heat a large frying pan, add the butter and sage and cook until the sage is crisp and the butter is foaming but not colouring. Throw in your drained tortellini and squeeze in some of the lemon juice to taste. Serve immediately and sprinkle generously with the remaining Parmesan.

I–Thai fried tortellini of chicken, ginger, water chestnut and lemon grass with dipping sauce

This is a bastardization of the fantastic *gyozas* (Japanese dumplings) served at Wagamama bistros in London. They can even be deep fried for a really mad crispy texture. It's fine to improvise, using prawns, pork or vegetables in the filling.

serves 6
a couple of thumb-sized pieces of fresh ginger, peeled
2 cloves of garlic, peeled
3 sticks of lemon grass, outer leaves removed, chopped
4 legs of chicken, preferably organic, bone removed
2 good handfuls of fresh coriander, including stalks
2 tablespoons sesame seed oil
1 egg
2 heaped dessertspoons cornflour
2 handfuls of tinned water chestnuts
salt and freshly ground black pepper
1 × fresh pasta recipe (page 98)
olive oil

In a food processor finely whizz up your ginger, garlic and lemon grass. Add your chicken meat and whizz for a further minute. Add the rest of the ingredients except the pasta and pulse the food processor until you achieve an interesting, smoothish texture. Start to fill your tortellini with a teaspoon of filling (page 113). Once they are filled, cook them for 3–4 minutes in salted boiling water. Remove, drain and place the tortellini into a hot non-stick pan drizzled with a couple of lugs of olive oil. Fry until one side is crisp and golden, then remove straight away and serve with the dipping sauce.

tasty dipping sauce

You can vary this dipping sauce to your own preference, using things like kaffir lime leaves, lime juice and ginger as possibilities.

12 tablespoons soy sauce
4 tablespoons rice wine or white wine vinegar
2 teaspoons sugar
$\frac{1}{2}$ a fresh chilli, finely chopped
a little fresh coriander, chopped

Put all the ingredients into a bowl and stir. Divide into little dipping bowls to serve.

dried pasta

A lot of people think that fresh pasta is superior to dried – that's rubbish, it's just that they do different things. Dried pasta is generally made from flour and mostly water, which means that it lasts for ages and retains a fantastic bite which is great for seafood, oily and tomato sauces, whereas fresh pasta is silky and tender and suits being stuffed and served with creamy and buttery sauces. Here are some of my favourite dried pasta recipes.

spaghetti with squashed olives, tomatoes, garlic, olive oil and chopped rocket

serves 4

olive oil

1 clove of garlic, finely chopped

1 small dried chilli, to taste

3 good handfuls of cherry or plum tomatoes,
   deseeded and roughly chopped

1 good handful of olives, squashed and destoned

455g/1lb dried spaghetti, the best you can get

salt and freshly ground black pepper

3 good handfuls of rocket, roughly chopped

Heat up a large frying pan, add a couple of good lugs of olive oil and fry the garlic and chilli for 30 seconds before adding the tomatoes and olives. Toss over and allow to cook for a further 4–6 minutes. Meanwhile, cook your spaghetti in salted boiling water until al dente. The tomatoes will thicken into a lovely sauce with some nice fresh chunks in it as well. Toss over and add to your drained pasta. Season to taste.

Add the chopped rocket, toss quickly, and serve in a big bowl immediately. Don't waste any time – get it on the table, let people help themselves and have a nice big green salad, a bit of bread and some wine. Lovely, fantastic.

spaghetti with olive oil, garlic, chilli and parsley

serves 4
455g/1lb dried spaghetti, the best you can get
1 large clove of garlic, finely chopped
olive oil
1–2 fresh red chillies, deseeded and finely chopped
1 good handful of flat-leaf parsley, finely chopped
salt and freshly ground black pepper

While cooking the spaghetti in salted boiling water until al dente, fry the garlic in a couple of good lugs of olive oil until softened. Add your chillies, drained pasta and parsley. Toss over to coat, season and serve.

spaghetti with red onions, sun-dried tomatoes, balsamic vinegar and basil

serves 4
455g/1lb dried spaghetti, the best you can get
1 red onion, peeled and finely chopped
olive oil
2 handfuls of sun-dried tomatoes in oil, chopped
3 tablespoons balsamic vinegar
salt and freshly ground black pepper
2 handfuls of basil, torn
1 small handful of Parmesan or pecorino cheese, grated

While cooking the spaghetti in salted boiling water until al dente, slowly fry the onion in a couple of lugs of olive oil for 5 minutes until soft and tender. Stir in the tomatoes and vinegar, and throw in your drained pasta. Season and toss together with the basil. Serve with grated Parmesan or pecorino.

spaghetti with anchovies, dried chilli and pangritata

Pangritata is great. It's basically fried or toasted breadcrumbs in garlic oil. In Italy, pangritata was once used as a substitute for Parmesan, which some people couldn't afford. It gives a dish an excellent texture and crunch and, if made well, great flavour.

serves 4
455g/1lb dried spaghetti, the best you can get
6 tablespoons extra virgin olive oil
2 cloves of garlic, finely chopped
16 anchovy fillets
juice of 2 lemons
2 small dried red chillies, crumbled

for the pangritata
8 tablespoons olive oil
1 clove of garlic, sliced
1 good handful of fresh thyme, leaves picked
200g/7oz fresh breadcrumbs
salt and freshly ground black pepper

First make the pangritata. Put the olive oil into a hot thick-bottomed pan. Add the garlic, thyme and breadcrumbs; they will fry and begin to toast. Stir for a couple of minutes until the breadcrumbs are really crisp and golden. Season with a little salt and freshly ground black pepper and drain on kitchen paper.

Cook the spaghetti in salted boiling water until al dente. While it is cooking, put the oil and garlic in a pan and heat gently. As the garlic begins to soften, lay the anchovy fillets over the top. After a minute you will see them begin to melt. Squeeze in the lemon juice and sprinkle in the dried chillies. Toss in the drained spaghetti and coat it in the sauce. Taste a bit of pasta – it may need a little more lemon juice and a little extra seasoning. Serve straight away, sprinkled really generously with the pangritata.

linguine with pancetta, olive oil, chilli, clams and white wine

serves 4

455g/1lb dried linguine, the best you can get

olive oil

4 rashers of pancetta or dry-cured smoky bacon, sliced thinly

1 large clove of garlic, finely chopped

1–2 dried red chillies, crumbled

680g/1½ lb clams

2 glasses of white wine

1 good handful of parsley, roughly chopped

salt and freshly ground black pepper

Cook your linguine in salted boiling water until al dente. Meanwhile, get a pan hot and add a couple of good lugs of olive oil and the pancetta. Fry until golden, then add the garlic and chillies. Soften slightly and add the clams. Stir, then add the white wine. Put a lid on the pan and cook for a further couple of minutes until all the clams have opened – discard any that remain closed. Remove from the heat and add the drained linguine. Stir in the parsley, correct the seasoning and serve with all the cooking juices.

linguine puttanesca

serves 4

455g/1lb dried linguine, the best you can get

3 cloves of garlic, finely chopped

2–3 small dried red chillies, crumbled

1 teaspoon dried oregano

extra virgin olive oil

2 × 400g tins of tomatoes, drained and chopped

2 handfuls of big black olives, destoned

1 handful of capers, soaked in water and drained

12 anchovy fillets, roughly chopped

1 good handful of fresh basil

salt and freshly ground black pepper

Cook your linguine in salted boiling water until al dente. Meanwhile fry the garlic, chillies and oregano in a little olive oil until slightly softened. Add the tomatoes and bring to a simmer. Add the olives, capers and anchovies and continue to cook for about another 4 or 5 minutes until you have a lovely tomato sauce consistency. Remove from the heat, plunge the drained linguine into it, toss it over and cover with the sauce. Rip over all the basil, correct the seasoning and drizzle with good extra virgin olive oil.

farfalle with broccoli, anchovies and chilli

serves 4
2 heads of broccoli
1 large clove of garlic, finely chopped
15 anchovy fillets
2–3 small dried red chillies, crumbled
olive oil
455g/1lb dried farfalle, the best you can get
salt and freshly ground black pepper
1 handful of pine nuts, lightly toasted

Remove the buds from the broccoli and trim, peel and finely chop the stalks. In a pan fry the garlic, anchovies, chillies and all the broccoli very slowly in a couple of lugs of olive oil for about 15 minutes with the lid on, adding a little water if need be. Feel free to mash some of the broccoli up as it cooks, giving you a chunky puréed sauce. Season to taste. Cook your farfalle in salted boiling water until al dente. Mix the drained pasta with your tasty sauce, adding a little cooking liquor to loosen if necessary, throwing in the pine nuts just before serving.

farfalle with Savoy cabbage, pancetta, thyme and mozzarella

serves 4

10 rashers of pancetta or dry-cured streaky bacon, thinly sliced

olive oil

1 clove of garlic, finely chopped

1 good handful of thyme, leaves picked

1 large Savoy cabbage (outer leaves removed),
   quartered, cored and finely sliced

1 handful of grated Parmesan cheese

455g/1lb dried farfalle, the best you can get

salt and freshly ground black pepper

extra virgin olive oil

200g/7oz buffalo mozzarella, cut into 1cm/$\frac{1}{2}$ inch dice

2 handfuls of pine nuts, lightly toasted

In a pan fry your pancetta in a little olive oil until lightly golden. Add the garlic and thyme and soften. Add the Savoy cabbage and Parmesan, then stir and put the lid on the pan. Cook for a further 5 minutes, shaking every now and again, while you cook your farfalle in salted boiling water until al dente. When the cabbage is nice and tender, season and loosen with some nice peppery extra virgin olive oil. Toss the drained farfalle into the cabbage and at the last minute mix in the mozzarella and pine nuts. Serve immediately.

return of the risotto

I think this is the best basic risotto recipe you will come across – you will find it really easy. I assure you that once you've got the knack you'll carry on making it all the time and it won't let you down. You can so easily enhance it by adding different seasonal ingredients. So here's the basic risotto, which will give you an amazingly creamy base, followed by some simple recipes to take the dish in completely different directions.

serves 6

approx. 1.1 litres/2 pints stock (chicken, fish or vegetable
   as appropriate – pages 275-6)
1 tablespoon olive oil
3 shallots or 2 medium onions, finely chopped
2 cloves of garlic, finely chopped
$1/2$ a head of celery, finely chopped
400g/14oz risotto rice
2 wine glasses of dry white vermouth (dry Martini or
   Noilly Prat) or dry white wine
Maldon sea salt and freshly ground black pepper
70g/2$1/2$oz butter
115g/4oz freshly grated Parmesan cheese

Stage 1

Heat the stock. In a separate pan heat the olive oil, add the shallots or onions, garlic and celery, and fry slowly for about 4 minutes. When the vegetables have softened, add the rice and turn up the heat.

Stage 2

The rice will now begin to fry, so keep stirring it. After a minute it will look slightly translucent. Add the vermouth or wine and keep stirring – it will smell fantastic. Any harsh alcohol flavours will evaporate and leave the rice with a tasty essence.

Stage 3

Once the vermouth or wine has cooked into the rice, add your first ladle of hot stock and a good pinch of salt. Turn down the heat to a highish simmer so the rice doesn't cook too quickly on the outside. Keep adding ladlefuls of stock, stirring and almost massaging the creamy starch from the rice, allowing each ladleful to be absorbed before adding the next. This will take around 15 minutes. Taste the rice – is it cooked?

Carry on adding stock until the rice is soft but with a slight *bite*. Don't forget to check the seasoning carefully.

Stage 4

Remove from the heat and add the butter and Parmesan. Stir gently. Place a lid on the pan and allow to sit for 2–3 minutes. This is the most important part of making the risotto, as this is when it becomes outrageously creamy and oozy like it should be. Eat as soon as possible while the risotto retains its perfect texture.

roasted sweet garlic, thyme and mascarpone risotto with toasted almonds and breadcrumbs

Don't be scared by this one – the garlic is not overpowering, it's an extremely subtle and delicate combination.

serves 6
1 × basic risotto recipe (pages 134–5)
2 large heads of garlic, whole and unpeeled
1 good handful of fresh thyme, leaves picked
155g/5¹/₂oz shelled and peeled almonds, lightly crushed,
    cracked or chopped
2 handfuls of coarse fresh breadcrumbs
olive oil
2 heaped tablespoons mascarpone cheese

Roast the whole garlic heads on a dish in the oven at 230°C/450°F/gas 8 for about 30 minutes until soft. Separate the cloves and squeeze out the sweet insides. Add with the thyme at the start of Stage 3 of the basic risotto recipe. In a frying pan toast the almonds and breadcrumbs in a little olive oil until crisp and golden. Season with a little salt. Set to one side. Serve the risotto with a dollop of mascarpone on the top and sprinkle over the toasted almonds and breadcrumbs. Lovely.

white risotto with lemon thyme, sliced prosciutto, pecorino and crumbled goat's cheese

I initially made this risotto pretty much off the cuff with leftover cheese from my fridge and a snip of lemon thyme from my window-box. It was perfect. Use normal thyme if you cannot get hold of lemon thyme.

serves 6
1 × basic risotto recipe (pages 134–5)
2 good handfuls of fresh lemon thyme, leaves picked
115g/4oz pecorino cheese, grated
155g/5½oz goat's cheese, crumbled
8 slices prosciutto

At the start of Stage 3 of the basic risotto recipe add the lemon thyme. When you stir in your butter and Parmesan at Stage 4, add the pecorino. Lay over the prosciutto slices just before eating and serve with the goat's cheese crumbled over the top. Scatter with a little extra thyme leaves if you like.

prawn and pea risotto with basil and mint

For me this risotto really works because of the natural sweetness you get in peas and prawns. With a little help from some delicate herbs it will put a smile on your face. Remember not to use any Parmesan in your basic risotto recipe – not good with fish. If using fresh peas, add the pods to the stock to give it a good pea flavour rather than throw them away. Results with good frozen peas are also brilliant.

serves 6
1 × basic risotto recipe (pages 134–5)
3 good handfuls of fresh peas, podded
1 knob of butter
455g/1lb raw prawns, peeled
1 handful of fresh basil, chopped
$^{1}/_{2}$ a handful of fresh mint, chopped
juice of 1 lemon
extra virgin olive oil

Fry half the peas in a good knob of butter and a little stock. Cook until tender and mash. Add this at the end of Stage 3 of the basic risotto recipe with the prawns and the rest of the peas and simmer for 2 minutes – prawns and peas take no time to cook. At Stage 4 throw in the fresh herbs and squeeze in the lemon juice. Stir and serve immediately. Drizzle with really nice peppery extra virgin olive oil.

risotto of radicchio, smoky bacon, rosemary and red wine

serves 6
1 × basic risotto recipe (pages 134–5)
3 wine glasses of your favourite full-bodied red wine
10 rashers of smoked streaky bacon, finely sliced
olive oil
2 heads of radicchio, trimmed and finely sliced
1 handful of fresh rosemary
1 small knob of butter

Add the red wine in place of the vermouth or white wine at Stage 2 of the basic risotto recipe. Fry your bacon in a little olive oil until slightly golden. Add the radicchio and rosemary to the pan with a small knob of butter and cook gently with the lid on until wilted. At the start of Stage 3 stir in the bacon, radicchio and rosemary.

joe

fish and shellfish

monkfish wrapped in banana leaves with ginger, coriander, chilli and coconut milk

You just can't go wrong with this combination of flavours. It's open to all white fish, especially swordfish, cod, haddock and monkfish. Banana leaves are very easy to buy from oriental stores. Get nice big ones to wrap your fish up in. Failing banana leaves, you can use vine leaves which you can get in the supermarkets – somewhat smaller, but no less tasty for that. If you really can't get hold of any leaves then kitchen foil will do.

serves 4

4 large banana leaves or vine leaves
a little olive oil
2 fresh chillies, red, green or both
2 sticks of lemon grass, outer leaves removed, finely chopped
1 clove of garlic, finely chopped
2 good handfuls of fresh coriander, roughly chopped
juice and zest of 2 limes
2 tablespoons sesame seed oil
2 heaped tablespoons finely sliced fresh ginger
170–225g/6–8oz monkfish per person
1 × 400ml tin of coconut milk
4 rosemary sprigs or bay leaf sticks, to secure

Preheat the oven to 230°C/450°F/gas 8. Lay out your banana leaves and rub them with olive oil. Leaving aside your fish, coconut milk and herb sticks, sprinkle a little bit of everything else on one end of each leaf. Place your fish on top and then sprinkle what's left over them. Pour 5–6 tablespoons of coconut milk into each parcel before folding the leaf over the fish, bringing the sides in and spiking it with a rosemary sprig or bay leaf stick to secure it. This will look lovely and it's natural, but I have been known to use a clothes peg or string to hold it all together. It won't be a perfect seal but this allows it to breathe and steam, letting the flavours infuse. So gutsy and tasty. Put your parcels on a tray and bake for 15 minutes, then remove from the oven and allow to rest for 5 minutes.

I serve the individual parcels on plates at the table and let my friends dissect them. When opened, the fragrant steam wafts up and smells fantastic. Serve with plain boiled rice to mop up the juices – that's all it has to be. End of story, done, lovely.

tray-baked cod with runner beans, pancetta and pine nuts

Another superb combination. The runner beans, pancetta and pine nuts go amazingly well together. It's a great way to cook the cod because it's all in one tray, which means hardly any washing up.

serves 4
680g/1½lb runner beans, trimmed and sliced at an angle
1 clove of garlic, finely sliced
salt and freshly ground black pepper
olive oil
4 × 225g/8oz cod steaks, on the bone
12 slices of smoked pancetta or streaky bacon
1 good handful of pine nuts
2 lemons, halved

Preheat the oven to 220°C/425°F/gas 7. Place your runner beans in an appropriately sized roasting tin. Throw in your garlic and a little salt and pepper, add just enough olive oil to coat the beans, and mix it all around. Nestle the cod steaks in among the runner beans, lightly season again, and then place some pancetta over the cod and among the beans. Sprinkle with pine nuts and drizzle a little olive oil over the top. Take your lemon halves and place them in the tray – they will cook and colour slightly, going jammy, sweet and lemony. Fantastic.

Cook for roughly 15 minutes in the middle of the preheated oven. Lightly lay kitchen foil over the fish for the first 5 minutes and then remove it. You know the cod is cooked when the bone in the middle is easily removed. This is a meal in itself, so serve with all the lovely juices from the tray drizzled over the top.

whole sea bass baked in a bag and stuffed with herbs

This is a great way to cook fish, letting it retain all its natural juices and moisture and rewarding you with the most fantastic tasty sauce. I think the fish is best served in its bag in the middle of the table – it's real theatre. When the bag is broken open the fragrant smells waft all around the table, leaving everyone salivating for it.

serves 4

1 × 1.8kg/4lb sea bass or 2 × 900g/2lb sea bass, scaled and gutted

1 red onion, peeled and finely sliced

1 bulb of fennel, finely sliced

1 clove of garlic, peeled and finely chopped

sea salt and freshly ground black pepper

1 dessertspoon fennel seeds

4 handfuls of mixed fresh herbs

   (parsley, basil, fennel, dill, tarragon, marjoram, bay)

3 lemons

6 good lugs of extra virgin olive oil

Preheat the oven to 220°C/425°F/gas 7. Tear off a piece of kitchen foil 5 times as long as your fish, then fold this in half to give you double thickness. In the middle of one half of the foil sprinkle the red onion, fennel and garlic. Place your fish snugly on top of the veg. Season the inside and outside of the fish with sea salt, freshly ground black pepper and the fennel seeds, then stuff with all your herbs – use just one herb or a mixture of your favourites. Squeeze over the juice of 2 of the lemons, slice the third lemon and tuck around the fish, and pour over the olive oil.

   Fold the foil over the fish and seal the three edges neatly and tightly, being careful not to pierce the foil as this will let the juices escape. Cook in the preheated oven for 10 minutes per 455g/1lb. If using a 1.8kg/4lb fish, then obviously give it 40 minutes, if using 2 two-pounders (900g) then you only need to cook them for 20 minutes. Once removed from the oven, allow the fish to rest for 5 minutes before serving at the table. Nice with simple boiled potatoes and a crisp salad.

wok-cooked fragrant mussels

I had the idea for this dish while eating mussels in New York. It takes literally minutes to cook and tastes absolutely pukka. Simply serve with plain boiled or steamed rice.

serves 4-6
2 kg/4¹/₂lb best live mussels, debearded
olive oil
2 cloves of garlic, finely sliced
3 sticks of lemon grass, outer leaves removed, finely sliced
2 fresh chillies, red, green or both
3 tablespoons finely sliced ginger
2 handfuls of fresh coriander, pounded or finely chopped
1 tablespoon sesame seed oil
salt and freshly ground black pepper
5 spring onions, finely sliced
juice of 3 limes
1 × 400ml tin of coconut milk

Place your mussels with a couple of lugs of olive oil in a large, very hot wok or pot. Shake around and add the rest of the ingredients, apart from the lime juice and coconut milk. Keep turning over until all the mussels have opened – throw away any that remain closed. Squeeze in your lime juice and add your coconut milk. Bring to the boil and serve immediately.

roasted slashed fillet of sea bass stuffed with herbs, baked on mushroom potatoes with salsa verde – à la Tony Blair

I cooked this for Tony Blair and the Italian prime minister at the British/Italian summit last year. It went down a treat so I thought I'd put it in the book. This is a really great way to cook sea bass. Try to get the fattest bass fillets you can find. Failing that, royal bream is fantastic cooked this way too.

serves 4

4 × 225g/8oz sea bass fillets
1 handful of mixed herbs (green or purple basil, flat-leaf
    parsley, thyme), roughly chopped
1kg/2lb 3oz potatoes, scrubbed
olive oil
2 cloves of garlic, finely chopped
salt and freshly ground black pepper
3 knobs of butter
455g/1lb mixed, preferably wild, mushrooms, torn
3 lemons
1 × salsa verde recipe (page 277)

Preheat the oven to 240°C/475°F/gas 9. Put a bit of greaseproof paper on the bottom of a baking tray, rubbed with olive oil. Slash the fish fillets about half-way down and stuff the slashes with the herbs. Slice the potatoes lengthways, just under 1cm/½ inch thick. Dry them off with kitchen paper and very lightly coat them in olive oil. Mix in half of your garlic, season with salt and pepper, then lay them out in one layer on the tray. Cook the potatoes in the oven for around 15 minutes until just cooked. Remove and put to one side.

Put the rest of the garlic into a pan with 2 good knobs of butter and a lug of olive oil. Fry your mixed mushrooms and season until tasty. If water comes out of them just continue cooking until it evaporates. Take the pan off the heat, squeeze in the juice from 1 lemon and stir in another knob of butter. Now scatter the mushrooms over the potatoes and kind of rub them in on top, underneath, all over. Place your sea bass fillets on top. Now bake in the oven for 12–15 minutes, depending on the thickness of your fish.

Remove the tray from the oven, put some kitchen foil over the top and let it sit for about 5 minutes, during which time all the lovely juices will run out into the potatoes. Serve it with salsa verde, half a lemon each and a glass of crisp white wine.

fantastic fish pie

The whole fish pie thing is one of the most homely, comforting and moreish dinners I can think of. This is a cracking recipe which does it for me.

serves 6

5 large potatoes, peeled and diced into 2.5cm/1 inch squares
salt and freshly ground black pepper
2 free-range eggs
2 large handfuls of fresh spinach
1 onion, finely chopped
1 carrot, halved and finely chopped
extra virgin olive oil
approx. 285ml/1/2 pint double cream
2 good handfuls of grated mature Cheddar or Parmesan cheese
juice of 1 lemon
1 heaped teaspoon English mustard
1 large handful of flat-leaf parsley, finely chopped
455g/1lb haddock or cod fillet, skin removed,
    pin-boned and sliced into strips
nutmeg (optional)

Preheat the oven to 230°C/450°F/gas 8. Put the potatoes into salted boiling water and bring back to the boil for 2 minutes. Carefully add the eggs to the pan and cook for a further 8 minutes until hard-boiled, by which time the potatoes should also be cooked. At the same time, steam the spinach in a colander above the pan. This will only take a minute. When the spinach is done, remove from the colander and gently squeeze any excess moisture away. Then drain the potatoes in the colander. Remove the eggs, cool under cold water, then peel and quarter them. Place to one side.

In a separate pan slowly fry the onion and carrot in a little olive oil for about 5 minutes, then add the double cream and bring just to the boil. Remove from the heat and add the cheese, lemon juice, mustard and parsley. Put the spinach, fish and eggs into an appropriately sized earthenware dish and mix together, pouring over the creamy vegetable sauce. The cooked potatoes should be drained and mashed — add a bit of olive oil, salt, pepper and a touch of nutmeg if you like. Spread on top of the fish. Don't bother piping it to make it look pretty — it's a homely hearty thing. Place in the oven for about 25–30 minutes until the potatoes are golden. Serve with some nice peas or greens, not forgetting your baked beans and tomato ketchup. Tacky but tasty and that's what I like.

seared scallops and crispy prosciutto with roasted tomatoes and smashed white beans

serves 4

4 large ripe plum tomatoes, quartered
salt and freshly ground black pepper
a pinch of dried oregano
olive oil
8 slices of prosciutto
1 small clove of garlic, finely chopped
1–2 small dried red chillies, crumbled to taste
4–6 anchovy fillets, chopped
1 × 400g tin of cannellini beans or flageolet beans, drained
extra virgin olive oil
12–16 scallops, trimmed with roe on or off to your preference
1 × olive oil and lemon juice dressing (page 81)
a small handful of peppery leaves (rocket or watercress)

Preheat the oven to 240°C/475°F/gas 9. Season the tomatoes and sprinkle with the oregano. Drizzle with olive oil and roast in the oven skin side down for about 10–15 minutes. Place the prosciutto slices beside the tomatoes and continue to roast for a further 10 minutes until the tomatoes are juicy and the prosciutto is crisp. In a pan fry the garlic, chillies and anchovies in a lug of olive oil for a minute or so. Add your beans and cook for a couple of minutes before adding a wine glass of water. Bring to the boil, then lightly mash to a coarse purée. Loosen the purée with a little more water if need be. Finish the flavour off with some peppery extra virgin olive oil, salt and freshly ground black pepper.

Season the scallops then sear them in a frying pan with a touch of olive oil for 2 minutes without touching them. Check and continue to fry until they have a lovely sweet caramelized skin – turn them over and allow the other side to do the same. Don't overcook them. Remove to a bowl and coat with a little olive oil and lemon juice dressing. Put some smashed bean purée on each plate, scatter over the tomatoes, prosciutto and scallops, and finish off with some peppery leaves.

baked trout and potatoes with a crème fraîche, walnut and horseradish sauce

Trout is a fantastic and readily available fish. The combination of hot horseradish, nutty walnuts and creamy crème fraîche is a pukka marriage with trout as well as with the more obvious beef and lamb.

serves 4
455g/1lb potatoes, peeled and finely sliced
olive oil
salt and freshly ground black pepper
4 whole trout, approx. 400–455g/14oz–1lb each,
    gutted and scaled
1 heaped tablespoon grated fresh horseradish
255g/9oz crème fraîche
2 handfuls of fresh walnuts, shelled and crushed
juice of 1 lemon

optional
a little fresh thyme, leaves picked
1 lemon, sliced

Preheat the oven to 240°C/475°F/gas 9. Dry your sliced potatoes with kitchen paper and lightly coat in olive oil. Season and place in a single layer in a large roasting tray. Place on a low oven shelf and roast for around 15 minutes, until crisp and golden. Meanwhile pat the trout dry, then with a sharp knife slash each fish at an angle on both sides – this will allow the heat and seasoning to penetrate. Rub with olive oil and seasoning. For extra flavour you can stuff the fish with fragrant herbs. I like to use thyme with some lemon slices too. This should only take a couple of minutes. Cook for around 12 minutes at the top of the oven until crisp and golden.

While the fish and potatoes are cooking make your sauce. Fresh horseradish, which you should peel and grate, is nicer, but you can also use the creamed horseradish bought in jars. Not quite as hot but still tasty. Mix the horseradish in a bowl with the crème fraîche and the walnuts and season well. Squeeze over some lemon juice to taste.

Serve the fish and potatoes side by side with a good lob of the crème fraîche sauce. Really nice with a green salad, some buttered bread and a glass of beer.

grilled swordfish, green beans and spicy tomato salsa

serves 4

4 × 170–225g/6–8oz swordfish steaks (1cm/½ inch thick)

olive oil

salt and freshly ground black pepper

5 handfuls of mixed salad leaves (watercress, rocket,
    radicchio, chicory, dandelion)

2 handfuls of green beans, cooked until tender

1 x olive oil and lemon juice dressing (page 81)

1 x tomato salsa recipe (page 277)

Rub the swordfish steaks with a little bit of olive oil, salt and freshly ground black pepper. Place on a very hot ridged griddle pan or barbecue and char for 2 minutes on each side. Remove from the pan. Lightly dress the beans and salad leaves with the olive oil and lemon juice dressing. Rip up the swordfish and place it in and among the beans and salad leaves. Smear over the spicy tomato salsa before serving.

wok-fried crispy bream with steamed greens and Thai dressing

serves 2

2 × 285–400g/10–14oz royal or grey bream

2 × Asian marinade (page 194)

sunflower oil

flour, for dusting

2 good handfuls of Chinese greens
   (spinach, pak choi, bok choi, Chinese broccoli)

1 × Thai dressing (page 80)

Slash the bream on both sides, about 1cm/¹⁄₂ inch deep, in a criss-cross fashion. In a pestle and mortar pound up the marinade and rub it into the fish, getting it into the cuts and the belly. Let this sit for up to an hour.

Heat a wok with about 5–7.5cm/2–3 inches of sunflower oil in. Put a bit of potato into the oil and when it is nicely golden you know the wok is hot enough – be very careful with the hot oil. Remove the bream from the marinade and pat dry with kitchen paper. Dust each fish with flour, shaking off any excess. Then carefully place each fish into the wok and fry for 3 minutes on each side. The skin will go amazingly crispy. Steam the greens in a colander above boiling water until tender. To serve, place the greens on a plate, put the fish on top, and smear and drizzle with the Thai dressing.

salmon fillet wrapped in prosciutto with herby lentils, spinach and yoghurt

serves 4
255g/9oz lentils
4 × 225g/8oz salmon fillets, skinned and pin-boned
salt and freshly ground black pepper
8 slices of prosciutto
olive oil
juice of 1 lemon
2 good handfuls of mixed herbs (flat-leaf parsley, basil, mint), chopped
3 large handfuls of spinach, chopped
200ml/7fl oz natural yoghurt

Preheat the oven to 220°C/425°F/gas 7. Put the lentils into a pan, cover with water, bring to the boil and simmer until tender. Season the salmon fillets with a little pepper before wrapping them in the prosciutto slices. Leave some of the flesh exposed. Drizzle with olive oil and roast in the oven for around 10 minutes until the prosciutto is golden. Feel free to cook the salmon for less time if pinker is to your liking. Drain away most of the water from the lentils and season carefully with salt, pepper, the lemon juice and 4 good lugs of olive oil. Just before serving, stir the herbs and spinach into the lentils on a high heat, until wilted. Place on to plates with the salmon and finish with a drizzle of lightly seasoned yoghurt.

**meat,
poultry
and game**

roast loin of pork with peaches

Pork, peaches, butter and thyme is one of the most luscious combinations I've ever had. You must try it.

serves 6
1 × 7-rib loin of pork, preferably organic
1 bunch of fresh thyme, leaves picked and chopped
200g/7oz butter
salt and freshly ground black pepper
8 fresh peaches (or use 2 tins in natural juice), halved and stoned

Preheat the oven to 220°C/425°F/gas 7. Score the skin of your pork about 1cm/½ inch apart through the fat nearly to the meat. With a knife carefully part the meat from the ribs. Scrunch your chopped thyme into the butter with the seasoning. Rub and distribute a little of the butter into the gap you have made between the ribs and the meat. Push in as many peaches as you can fit and pack the rest of the butter on top. To hug the meat and ribs together and hold the peaches in place, simply fasten some string around the pork loin in 3 or 4 places and tie firmly. Place in a roasting tray with any leftover peaches and other veg you wish to cook with it – potatoes, parsnips, celeriac and Jerusalem artichokes are all good – and cook for 50 minutes to 1 hour, allowing it to rest for 10 minutes before serving. I usually make a little bit of homemade gravy in the roasting tray after removing the pork and veg. The sticky, marmitey goodness is great when boiled with a little water or wine and any extra juices from the pork. Tasty.

braised five hour lamb with wine, veg and all that

This is a real hearty and trouble-free dinner. There's barely any preparation, just a nice long cooking time which will reward you with the most tender meat and tasty sauce. Large legs of lamb are ideal for this dish as they benefit from slow cooking. If using a smaller leg of spring lamb then consider cooking for an hour less.

serves 6
1 large leg of lamb
salt and freshly ground black pepper
olive oil
6 rashers of thick streaky bacon
3 red onions, peeled and quartered
3 cloves of garlic, peeled and sliced
2 good handfuls of mixed fresh herbs (thyme, rosemary, bay)
4 large potatoes, peeled and cut into chunks
1 celeriac, peeled and cut into chunks
6 large carrots, scrubbed and halved
3 parsnips, scrubbed and halved
1 bottle of white wine

Preheat the oven to 170°C/325°F/gas 3. In a large casserole pot or a deep-sided roasting tray, fry your well-seasoned lamb in a couple of good lugs of olive oil until brown on all sides. Add the bacon, onions and garlic and continue to fry for 3 more minutes. Throw in your herbs and veg, pour in your wine plus an equivalent amount of water, bring to the boil, and tightly cover with kitchen foil. Bake in the preheated oven for 5 hours until tender, seasoning the cooking liquor to taste. To serve, pull away a nice portion of meat, take a selection of veg and serve with some crusty bread to mop up the gravy.

seared encrusted carpaccio of beef

The reason I like to make this dish is because, apart from being really quick and simple, it's a sociable feast where everyone can tuck in and help themselves. I love all that. I always serve this on a large plate in the middle of the table, with crusty bread and a glass of wine. Any leftovers are even more gorgeous the next day in a nice firm bap.

A good carpaccio is always made from a prime cut of meat or fish, like fillet or loin, and it is normally served completely rare. To make it different I sear it lightly, encrusting a fantastic flavour on the outside but still leaving it delicately and classically raw.

Here I will show you how to sear a fillet of beef with a tasty crust, followed by two of my favourite ways of serving it.

serves 6
1 heaped tablespoon coriander seeds, smashed
1 handful of fresh rosemary, finely chopped
salt and freshly ground black pepper
a light sprinkling of dried oregano
1.5kg/3¹/₂lb fillet of beef

Pound the coriander seeds in a pestle and mortar, then mix in the rosemary, salt, pepper and oregano and sprinkle on to a board. Roll and press the fillet of beef over this, making sure all the mixture sticks to the meat. In a very hot, ridged pan, or on a barbecue, sear the meat for around 5 minutes until brown and slightly crisp on all sides. Remove from the pan. Allow it to rest for 5 minutes, then slice it all up as thinly as you can. Lay the slices on a large plate.

seared carpaccio of beef with roasted baby beets, creamed horseradish, watercress and Parmesan

serves 6–8
680g/1½lb baby beetroots
olive oil
approx. 10 tablespoons balsamic vinegar
salt and freshly ground black pepper
1.5kg/3½lb fillet of beef
100g/3½oz freshly grated or creamed horseradish
200g/7oz crème fraîche
a splash of white wine vinegar
juice of 1 lemon
3 good handfuls of watercress
100g/3½oz shaved Parmesan cheese

Preheat the oven to 230°C/450°F/gas 8. Wash and scrub the beets, trim the ends, and toss into a roasting tray with a little oil, balsamic vinegar and seasoning. Cover with kitchen foil and roast until tender. Cooking time depends on size.

After preparing the beef (see page 175), sprinkle the roasted beetroots randomly (whole, halved or quartered, depending on size) over the sliced meat. Now mix your horseradish and crème fraîche together. It has to be seasoned well, usually needing a little white wine vinegar or lemon juice. Dribble this over the beetroots. Dress some watercress with olive oil and lemon juice. Then scatter this, along with some small slivers of shaved Parmesan, all over the plate and get ready to tuck in!

seared carpaccio of beef with chilli, ginger, radish and soy

This is really good served with crunchy Thai salad (see page 67) and some crusty bread.

serves 6–8
1.5kg/3½lb fillet of beef
1 handful of very finely sliced fresh ginger
   (preferably younger, unstringy stems)
2–3 fresh red or green chillies (or use a mixture of both),
   deseeded and finely sliced
1 good handful of radishes, finely sliced
1 small handful of fresh coriander, leaves picked,
   stalks finely sliced lengthwise
sesame seed oil
soy sauce
juice of 2 limes

After preparing the beef (see page 175), gather your ginger slices and cut finely across into little delicate matchsticks. Flick these randomly over the beef with the chillies, radishes and coriander. Drizzle with a very small amount of sesame seed oil, some soy sauce and your freshly squeezed lime juice, making sure each slice of meat gets an equal dousing.

tray-baked pork chops with herby potatoes, parsnips, pears and minted bread sauce

When I make this dish I ask my butcher to slice me a two-rib pork chop. I then ask him to lose one of the ribs and a little of the fat and to bat the meat out slightly, leaving me with a huge pork chop that looks fantastic.

serves 4
8 pork chops, or 4 double pork chops
1 × rosemary, garlic and lemon marinade (page 194)
3 parsnips
3 smooth-skinned pears
680g/1½lb potatoes, scrubbed
salt and freshly ground black pepper
1 × minted bread sauce recipe (page 278)

Rub and massage the pork chops with the rosemary marinade and, ideally, leave for 1–6 hours for maximum flavour. Preheat the oven to 220°C/425°F/gas 7. Wash the parsnips and pears and slice into quarters lengthwise, removing the cores from the pears, then cut the potatoes into 0.5cm/¼ inch thick pieces. Dry them with kitchen paper, then put them into an appropriately sized roasting tray with the parsnips, pears, pork chops and the marinade. Toss over to lightly coat everything then season and roast in the oven for 45 minutes to an hour, depending on the size of the chops.

While the chops and veg are cooking, make the minted bread sauce. It's great smeared all over the pork.

roasted Hamilton poussin wrapped with streaky bacon and stuffed with potatoes and sage

This is nothing to do with the Duke of Hamilton. It's a scrumptious recipe that my handsome art director Johnny Boy Hamilton cooks for his lovely wife. Lucky woman. There is something quite cute about the individual chicken thing, and cooking the potatoes in the cavities seems to make them taste even better.

serves 4
455g/1lb potatoes, peeled and quartered
sea salt and freshly ground black pepper
4 poussin chickens
1 handful of fresh sage, thyme or rosemary (all are good)
olive oil
about 12 cloves of garlic
12 rashers of dry-cured streaky bacon
1 glass of white wine

Preheat your oven and an appropriately sized roasting tray to 220°C/425°F/gas 7. Boil your potatoes in salted water until nearly cooked. Drain and allow to cool then put them in a bowl. Remove any fat from inside each chicken cavity. Wash and pat dry with kitchen paper. Season the potatoes with salt and freshly ground black pepper, add your freshly torn herbs and enough olive oil just to coat, and toss. Then stuff your chickens with half your potatoes and herbs. Put them in the hot roasting tray with the garlic and the rest of the potatoes and cook in the preheated oven for 30 minutes. After this time the chicken should be looking as handsome as its inventor and the skin should be crisp and golden. At this point lay your streaky bacon snugly over the breast meat. Cook for around another 15 minutes.

Remove the chickens from the oven. Take them out of the tray and allow them to rest for 5 minutes while you make a quick bit of gravy. I normally remove as much fat as possible from the tray before placing it on the hob on a gentle heat. Splash a glass of white wine into it. Then boil up and scrape away all the goodness from the sides of the tray. Simmer this for a couple of minutes. It's not a thick, robust gravy, just a tasty gesture. (A nice option at this point is to add a little cream to the gravy, which works really well.) Served with something nice and green like steamed spinach or chard, and the potatoes pulled out from inside the chickens, it all goes down a treat. Nice one, John.

fantastic roasted chicken

This roast chicken is really tasty. The principle is very similar to the perfect roast chicken recipe in my first book, getting fantastic flavours right into the bird.

serves 6
1.8kg/4lb chicken, preferably organic
1 large lemon
8 slices prosciutto or Parma ham, thinly sliced
1–2 cloves of garlic, peeled and finely chopped
2 good handfuls of fresh thyme, leaves picked and finely chopped
salt and freshly ground black pepper
115g/4oz or ½ pack of softened butter
1kg/2lb 3oz potatoes, peeled and cut into chunks
1 large celeriac, peeled

Preheat the oven and an appropriately sized roasting tray to 220°C/425°F/gas 7. Wash your chicken inside and out and pat dry with kitchen paper. Using your fingers, part the breast skin from the breast meat. It's important to try to push your hand gently down the breast, being careful not to rip the skin. With a peeler, remove and chop the fragrant yellow skin of the lemon, keeping the peeled lemon to one side. Then tear up your prosciutto and add to a bowl with the lemon skin, garlic and thyme. Season, and then scrunch it all into the butter. Push this into the space you have made between the meat and the skin – rub and massage any that's left over in and around the bird. It's all tasty stuff. I could tell you to tie the chicken up but I've decided it's a palaver and not worth it in this case. Slash the thigh meat to allow the heat to penetrate a little more, which makes it taste better. Cut the peeled lemon in half and push it into the cavity. Then put your chicken in the hot roasting tray and roast in the preheated oven for 25 minutes.

   While the chicken is cooking, parboil the potatoes in salted water for 10 minutes and drain. Cut the celeriac into irregular chunks around the same size as the potatoes. Remove the chicken from the oven, by which time the tasty butter will have melted, flavoured and cooked out of the chicken into the bottom of the tray, awaiting your potatoes and celeriac. Normally I put a fork into the cavity of the chicken and lift it out of the tray for 20 seconds while I toss and coat the vegetables in the butter. Put the chicken back on top of the vegetables and cook for around 45 minutes. Leave to stand for 10 minutes. Once the meat and vegetables have been removed, a little light gravy can be made in the tray on the hob with a splash of wine and stock, a little simmering and scraping.

roasted fillet of beef rolled in herbs and porcini and wrapped in prosciutto

As far as roasted meat goes, this is extremely fast and simple, yet decadently rich. One of the tricks, whether you buy it in a deli or a supermarket, is to ask them to slice your prosciutto and lay it side by side on to an A3 (ish) sized piece of waxed paper.

serves 4
12–18 slices prosciutto or Parma ham
3 cloves of garlic, peeled
1 good handful of dried porcini, soaked in around 285ml/½ pint boiling water
3 good knobs of butter
juice of ½ a lemon
sea salt and freshly ground black pepper
900g/2lb fillet of beef (preferably from the middle, left whole)
1 good handful of fresh rosemary and thyme, leaves picked and chopped
2 glasses of red wine

Preheat your oven and an appropriately sized roasting tray to 230°C/450°F/gas 8. Make sure there are no gaps in between the laid-out slices of prosciutto. Chop one of the garlic cloves and fry with the soaked porcini in 1 knob of butter for a minute. Then add half of the soaking water (make sure it is grit-free). Simmer slowly and reduce for around 5 minutes before stirring in a squeeze of lemon, the remaining 2 knobs of butter and seasoning. Rub your tasty and moist mushrooms over half of the laid-out prosciutto. Season your fillet of beef and roll it in the herbs. Place it on the mushroomy end of the prosciutto and slowly roll up the meat. Once the beef is rolled up, pull off the paper and push in the ends of the prosciutto to neaten. Lightly secure with 4 pieces of string. Chefs have a certain way of doing this, but as long as the string holds the meat together I don't care how you do it.

Place the fillet in the hot roasting tray with a couple of cloves of garlic and cook for 25–30 minutes (rare), 40 minutes (medium), 50 minutes (well-done) or 60 minutes (cremated!). Half-way through, add the wine to the tray. When the meat is done, remove it to a chopping board and leave it to rest for 5 minutes. Pour any juices back into the roasting tray. Simmer the juices on the hob, scraping all the goodness from the sides of the tray. Remove from the heat and serve as a light red wine gravy. Slice the fillet as thick or as thin as you like and serve with some potatoes or some gorgeous greens. I like to reserve a little of the cooked porcini to serve with my greens.

braised pigeon breasts with peas, lettuce and spring onions

You can use whole pigeons in this recipe, but I prefer to remove the bottom of each carcass with a knife or a pair of scissors to open and flatten them out like a book. The cooking time I have given is sufficient, but if you like your meat pink then feel free to lessen it.

serves 4
4 pigeons
salt and freshly ground black pepper
olive oil
1 bunch of spring onions, stalks chopped and bulbs left whole
1 clove of garlic, peeled and finely chopped
3 good knobs of butter
1 heaped tablespoon flour
795g–1kg/1¾lb–2lb 3oz peas, fresh or frozen
2 cos lettuces, quartered
1.1 litres/2 pints chicken or vegetable stock (pages 275–6)

Preheat the oven to 220°C/425°F/gas 7 and get a high-sided casserole pan or roasting tray hot on the hob. Season the pigeons, then place them skin side down in the hot pan with a little olive oil until lightly golden. Remove from the pan and fry the chopped spring onion stalks and garlic for 1 minute until slightly softened. Add your knobs of butter and the flour. Turn down the heat and cook for a further 3 minutes without colouring. Add your peas, spring onion bulbs, lettuce and enough stock to cover, then place the pigeons on top, skin side up. Cook in the preheated oven for 20 minutes. Remove from the oven and allow to sit for 5 minutes before serving.

Peter's lamb curry

My mate Peter Begg, lovely bloke, fine chef, thoroughbred Scotsman, kilt and no undies, makes the best curry and likes a cold beer. Say no more . . . love him.

serves 8

1 × hot and fragrant rub (page 195)
2 tablespoons butter
2 × 400g tins of chopped tomatoes
285ml/½ pint stock or water
1.5kg/3½lb leg of lamb, diced
1 handful of chopped mint and coriander
285ml/½ pint natural yoghurt
salt and freshly ground black pepper
lime juice to taste

curry paste

5cm/2 inches of fresh ginger, peeled
2 tennis-ball-sized red onions, peeled
10 cloves of garlic, peeled
2 fresh red chillies, with seeds
1 bunch of fresh coriander

Preheat your oven to 170°C/325°F/gas 3. Chop the paste ingredients roughly, add the toasted and ground rub mix and purée in a food processor. In a large casserole pan, fry the curry paste mixture in the butter until it goes golden, stirring regularly. Add the tomatoes and the stock or water. Bring to the boil, cover with kitchen foil and place in the oven for 1½ hours to intensify the flavours. Remove the foil and continue to simmer on the stove until it thickens. This is your basic curry sauce.

Fry the lamb in a little olive oil until golden, then add to the curry sauce and simmer for around 1 hour or until tender. Feel free to vary the curry by using diced chicken, prawns or paneer (see below), or vegetables like Swiss chard, spinach, peas, cauliflower, fried aubergine, okra, boiled potatoes, chickpeas or lentils. Sprinkle with chopped coriander and mint and stir in the yoghurt. Season to taste and add a good squeeze of lime juice. Serve with spiced breads, steamed basmati rice and lots and lots of cold beer!

paneer Indian cheese

In a thick-bottomed pan, bring 2 litres of full cream milk to the boil, remove from the heat and add a wine glass of white wine vinegar. Stir, then leave for 5 minutes. The milk will begin to curdle. Now pour it through a fine sieve or a colander lined with muslin. Allow the water to drain, then squeeze the remaining curd and chill in the fridge. Chop the cheese into thumb-sized pieces, fry in butter with a little chilli, garlic and sea salt and add to your curry.

steaks, chops, fillets, legs and breasts, tenderloins, whole birds and half birds, cutlets, noisettes, medallions and all that malarkey

Absolutely everyone cooks these cuts of meat week in, week out. Pork, lamb, beef, chicken: we all cook them. And the idea of the marinades and rubs on pages 194–5 is to give you 6 possible ways to flavour them – to give you options other than the plain old grilled chop. When you have marinated or rubbed your chosen meat, grill, fry or roast it in a hot oven until perfectly cooked and leave for 5 minutes before serving.

marinades and rubs

Each of the following marinades and rubs will make enough to flavour at least 6–8 portions of meat or fish. They are a fantastic way of flavouring a piece of meat, taking it in a whole new direction. They're also great tenderizers, helping to break down any tough sinews.

The following flavours are literally the tip of the iceberg. Feel free to vary them depending on what herbs, oils and ingredients you have available. I like to rub and massage the meat for a little while to really get the flavours in there. Sometimes I bash out pork chops so the surface area is a bit bigger, or even lightly score chicken to impregnate the flavour quicker. Marinate your meat for anything between 1 and 8 hours, but these marinades, when used on first-class pieces of meat, do work best when left all day. I wouldn't leave them for any longer than that. Get your meat in the marinade first thing before work and it will be ready to cook for dinner that night.

Rubs are great ways of simply and cheaply flavouring meat or fish as, generally, they're based around dried herbs and spices which are non-perishable. You can improvise and make up your own but the 3 on page 195 are the ones I use all the time.

Asian marinade

2 sticks of lemon grass, crushed and bruised
1 small handful of kaffir lime leaves, torn
2 tablespoons soy sauce
2 cloves of garlic, crushed
1 thumb-sized piece of ginger, peeled and chopped
1 fresh red chilli, finely chopped
2 limes, halved, juiced and skin squashed
10 good lugs of olive oil

Scrunch the whole lot together in a bowl and coat
over your chosen meat. Also works brilliantly with fish.

yoghurt, mint and lime marinade

1 × 500ml tub of natural organic yoghurt
2 good handfuls of fresh mint, chopped
zest and juice of 2 limes
1 tablespoon coriander seeds, crushed
salt and freshly ground black pepper
a couple of lugs of olive oil

Mix together the ingredients and smear over
your chosen meat before leaving it to marinate.

rosemary, garlic and lemon marinade

2 good handfuls of fresh rosemary, pounded
6 cloves of garlic, crushed
10 lugs of olive oil
3 lemons, halved, juiced and skin squashed
freshly ground black pepper

Mix everything together and massage on
to your chosen meat. Leave the meat in the
marinade until you're ready to cook it.

hot and fragrant rub

2 tablespoons fennel seeds
2 tablespoons cumin seeds
2 tablespoons coriander seeds
½ tablespoon fenugreek seeds
½ tablespoon black peppercorns
1 clove
½ a cinnamon stick
2 cardamom pods
salt and freshly ground black pepper

Lightly toast all the ingredients in a pan over a gentle heat
before pounding or crushing into a fine powder. This can then
be rubbed generously over your chosen meat.

fennel seed, thyme and garlic rub

4 tablespoons fennel seeds
2 good handfuls of fresh thyme
2 cloves of garlic
1 bay leaf, ripped
salt and freshly ground black pepper

Pound together and rub all over your chosen meat.

Cajun spicy rub

2 tablespoons paprika
2 tablespoons cayenne pepper
1 tablespoon black peppercorns, ground
2 cloves of garlic, peeled and crushed
3 tablespoons onion flakes
2 tablespoons dried oregano
salt

Pound all the ingredients together until you have a
powdery consistency and rub all over your chosen meat.

Botham burger

The good thing about burgers is you can make them thin and big, fat and big, or even turn them into meatballs. In the early days of the Cricketers, the pub where I grew up, I remember my dad used to serve a whopping great burger the size of a cricket-ball topped with a huge amount of Cheddar cheese and homemade tomato relish. He very classily called it the Botham burger. That's what I love about Essex boys – sheer taste. Feel free to add extra spices if that's what takes your fancy, but here's a really solid basic beefburger recipe. I never thought when I became a chef that I would come back round to respecting the famous beefburger. Unfortunately it hasn't been on the pub's menu for about ten years – what a shame. This might change Dad's mind.

makes 4 Botham burgers
1kg/2lb 3oz minced beef, preferably organic
2 medium red onions, finely chopped
2 eggs
1–2 handfuls of fresh breadcrumbs
1 tablespoon of coriander seeds, crushed
1 small pinch of cumin seeds, crushed
1 heaped teaspoon Dijon mustard
salt and freshly ground black pepper

Preheat the oven to 230°C/450°F/gas 8. Mix and scrunch all the ingredients together. Use the breadcrumbs as required to bind and lighten the mixture. Divide into 4, then gently and lightly mould and pack each burger together into smallish cricket-ball-sized shapes. Place in the oven and roast for 25 minutes, which should leave the middle slightly pink and the outsides nice and crispy. Serve with a griddled bun, a little salad, some gherkins, tomato salsa (page 278), a pint of Guinness and a bottle of ketchup. Howzat!

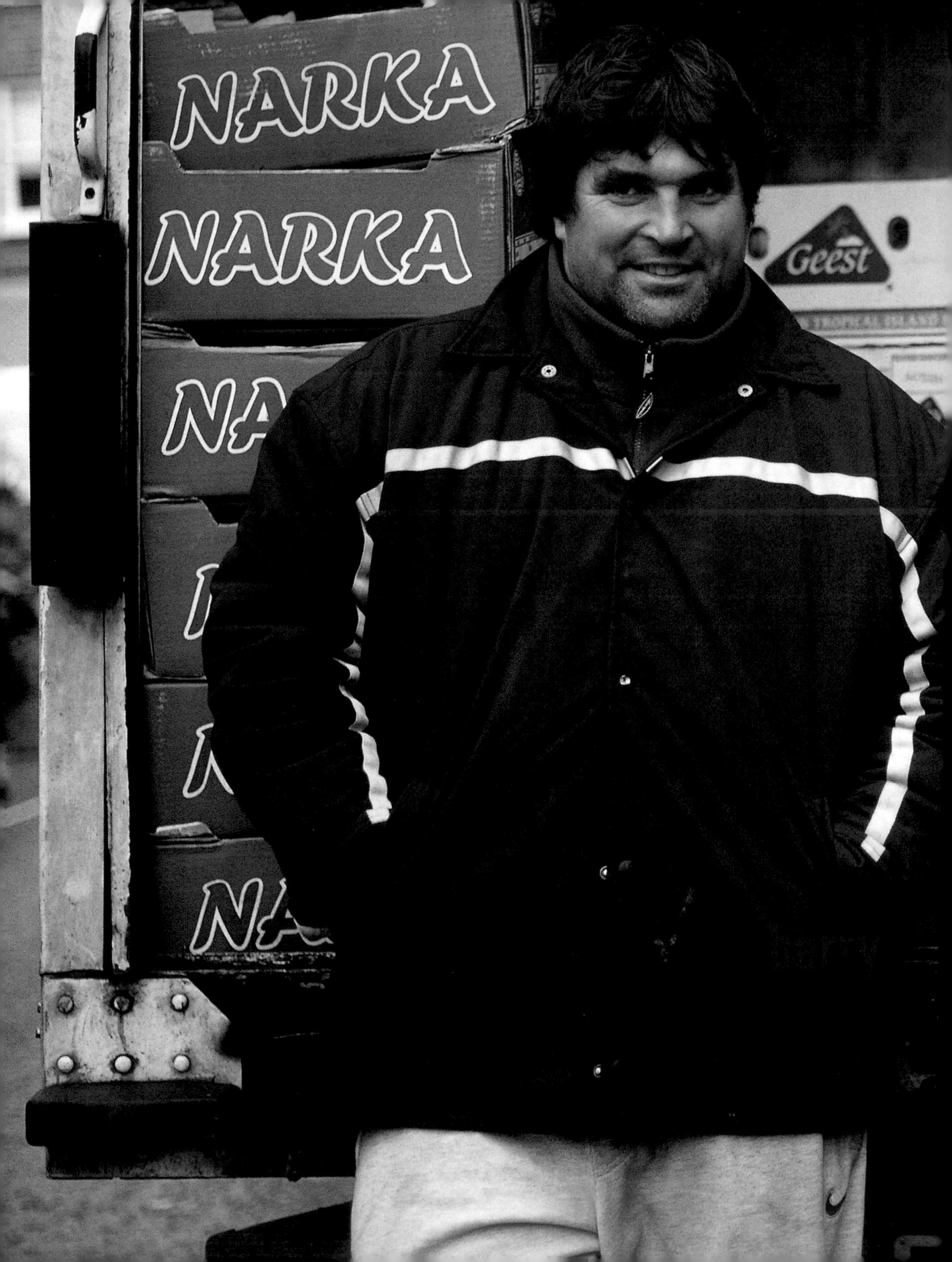
NARKA
NARKA
Geest

vegetables

Nothing much has changed in the veg world over the last year and a half, since my first book, but I still believe a lot of good things are going to happen in general supermarkets and markets. I've heard a few rumours that certain supermarkets think they're going to be 90 per cent organic by 2005, which is great. I wouldn't worry about price either, because as we buy more British produce, grown properly as it used to be before we started cheating and churning it out, it will become nice and cheap so everyone can afford it. Also, the variety of vegetables like cabbages, potatoes and tomatoes, as well as salad leaves, is slowly getting better. Things that could only be bought for restaurant use before are now popping up in supermarkets and that's superb.

I have noticed people's curiosity about cooking becoming more intense, which is great. I think a lot of people are now beginning to learn a lot about cooking and are really enjoying it, though sometimes when I walk round the supermarket I see such a massive contrast in buyers and I'm sure that will always be the case. In general I'll see young couples with their trolleys full of quite interesting vegetables – asparagus, artichokes, rocket – talking and sometimes arguing about the best combinations and ways to cook their veg for dinner. I find it so interesting. Usually they have some really good ideas, but others are definite no-nos and I do feel the urge to go up to them and say, 'Excuse me, I'm Dr Naked Chef, can I possibly help?' But I know they would just turn round and say, 'Who are you? On yer bike, mate!' The main thing, though, is that they are interested and they are trying. However, I can never get over the mother with lots of pasty kids and a trolley full of Coke, crisps and tinned spaghetti hoops. I feel like kidnapping the kids and force-feeding them vegetables for a month to get some colour back into their cheeks. There's no such thing as a vegetable that is too flashy or complicated for a kid. In Italy it is so common to see two-year-olds nibbling on asparagus tips and dipping artichoke hearts in flavoured butters and sauces. They love it, it's good fun and it's bloomin' good for them. At the end of the day, their diet is only as good as that of their parents.

baked endive with thyme, orange juice, garlic and butter

Five years on from swearing that I'd never eat another Belgian endive again, I'm writing a recipe for one that I think is gorgeous. Hypocritical I know, but there you go.

serves 4
4 Belgian endive
3 generous knobs of butter
1 clove of garlic, peeled and finely chopped
1 good handful of fresh thyme
salt and freshly ground black pepper
approx. 300ml/10–11fl oz fresh orange juice

Preheat the oven to 230°C/450°F/gas 7. Remove any discoloured outer leaves from the Belgian endive, if need be. Cut in half lengthways and then quarter each half. In a hot pan, fry the endive with your butter, garlic, thyme and seasoning for about 4 minutes. Add the orange juice and allow to sizzle. Then pour it all into a dish, cover with kitchen foil and bake for 10 minutes. Now remove the foil and bake for a further 10 minutes. Taste and correct your seasoning before serving.

baked fennel with garlic butter and vermouth

This dish is so quick. I made it the other day, chucked it together and it's really light and flavoursome. It goes fantastically well with any meat or fish.

serves 4
3 large heads of fennel
1 clove of garlic, finely sliced
3 large knobs of butter
2 wine glasses of vermouth (white wine also works)
salt and freshly ground black pepper

Preheat the oven to 220°C/425°F/gas 7. Remove any discoloured parts of the fennel, then cut the tops off and slice finely, reserving the leaves. I normally slice each fennel from the top to the root, into about 4 pieces, but it's not that important. You can slice them finer and more delicately if you like. Literally throw all the ingredients except the reserved leaves into a baking dish. Rip off a piece of greaseproof paper, run it under cold water and scrunch it up to make it soft. Then place it snugly over and around the fennel, not the actual dish. This bakes and steams the fennel at the same time — basically making it damn tasty! Cook in the preheated oven for 20 minutes, or until tender. Scatter with the fennel leaves before serving.

tray-baked field mushrooms studded with garlic and rubbed with butter and pounded thyme

In the restaurant we buy in some fantastic mushrooms, each with its own character, but they are very very expensive. With regard to mushrooms at home, stay a million miles away from the horrible boring button mushroom and go for the flat field mushroom. These vary in size, so I always buy ones as big as beer-mats. This recipe is absolutely fantastic, juicy and meaty.

serves 4
1 good handful of fresh thyme, leaves picked
a pinch of dried chilli
2 cloves of garlic, peeled and finely sliced
juice of 1 lemon
6 good lugs of extra virgin olive oil
4–8 flat field mushrooms, depending on size
1 knob of butter
salt and freshly ground black pepper

Preheat your oven to 220°C/425°F/gas 7. Pound up your thyme, chilli and a little of the garlic in a pestle and mortar. Squeeze in the lemon juice and add the olive oil. With your hand or a brush, rub the mushrooms all over with this mixture. Make sure all the flavoured oil is used up. Tightly pack the mushrooms together, bottom-side up, in an ovenproof dish or roasting tray, and with a knife make 2 to 3 little slits randomly over each one. Insert a slice of the remaining garlic into each slit. Dot the butter over the mushrooms, season, and bake for around 15–25 minutes – cooking time depends on the size of your mushrooms – until soft, slightly coloured and damn juicy. Taste one and see. Great served with steak and chips, ripped into a warm salad, chopped into ravioli, sliced and tossed with pasta and a bit of cream . . . nice one.

baked Jerusalem artichokes, breadcrumbs, thyme and lemon

This dish is absolutely spanking in the middle of your table for a Sunday roast or with a grilled bit of chicken or a pork chop. The breadcrumbs and thyme become crispy on top, giving the dish a really sexy texture of soft artichoke and crisp topping.

serves 4–6
285ml/¹/₂ pint double cream or crème fraîche
juice of 1 lemon
2 cloves of garlic, peeled and finely chopped
1 good handful of fresh thyme, leaves picked and chopped
3 handfuls of grated Parmesan cheese
salt and freshly ground black pepper
1kg/2lb 3oz Jerusalem artichokes, peeled and sliced
    as thick as a pencil
2 good handfuls of fresh breadcrumbs
olive oil

Preheat your oven to 220°C/425°F/gas 7. In a bowl mix your cream, lemon juice, garlic, half the thyme and most of the Parmesan, and season well to taste. Throw in the sliced Jerusalem artichokes. Mix well and place everything in an ovenproof baking dish.

Mix the breadcrumbs with the rest of the thyme and Parmesan and some salt and pepper. Sprinkle all the flavoured breadcrumbs over the artichokes and drizzle with a little olive oil. Bake in the oven for around 45 minutes until the artichokes are tender and the breadcrumbs are golden.

vegetables

good old spinach

I like the irony taste of
spinach, I love the colour, it's
really good for you but no one seems to know how
to cook it. My lovely mother-in-law boils the hell out
of it so she ends up with grey-green water and kinda
green spinach. Where's all the goodness?

In the water. So forget everything you know about cooking spinach, this is the way we do it from now on. Either pick or buy spinach on the stalk, which you should wash well, sometimes two or three times but that's not the end of the world. If you've got lovely young leaves then leave them on the stalk and just pick the outer leaves off. Or, as most of us do, buy packs of prewashed baby spinach from the supermarket – how convenient. Here are four brilliant ways with spinach. You can also use Swiss chard or Savoy cabbage in place of spinach.

the simplest spinach with nutmeg and butter

serves 4

To a hot pan or wok add a little oil, sway the pan about and add 4 huge handfuls of spinach. This will look like a lot, but it will soon cook down. It will sizzle a bit so just stand by it and turn it over every 5 seconds. After about 30 seconds it will begin to wilt and hopefully only a little water will start to cook out of the spinach (if there is a lot then pour a little away). Add 3 big knobs of butter and grate in about 12 rubs of nutmeg to taste. Mix, season and serve. The butter and the water should mix together giving you just enough natural sauce to bind everything together.

spinach and porcini with rosemary and lemon

serves 4

Dried porcini are everywhere now – too expensive, but the flavour is extreme and extraordinary. A small pack is more than enough for this recipe. Just cover the porcini with boiling water and soak for 15 minutes. Keeping the liquor to one side, fry the mushrooms with 2 large knobs of butter, 1 chopped clove of garlic and around 1 tablespoon of finely chopped rosemary. Fry for 4 minutes and then gently pour in around half of the soaking liquor – I say gently because sometimes a little grit falls to the bottom, which you don't want. Simmer the mushrooms until the butter and liquor have reduced just to coat them. Then plonk in 4 huge handfuls of spinach and mix round until the spinach is vibrant green and wilted. Season to taste with a squeeze of lemon, salt and freshly ground black pepper. An excellent filling for vegetarian cannelloni with a little ricotta.

spring onions, sweet peas, white wine and spinach

serves 4

In a pot slowly fry a handful of finely chopped spring onions for a couple of minutes in a lug of olive oil and a knob of butter. Then add 2 handfuls of fresh or frozen peas and cook for another couple of minutes before adding a good glass of white wine. Bring to the boil and simmer for a few minutes before adding 4 huge handfuls of spinach. Turn this over and cook until the spinach is wilted. Add 2 huge knobs of butter and season well to taste.

steamed spinach with coconut rice

serves 4
1 × 400ml tin of coconut milk
salt
400g/14oz long-grain rice
4 tablespoons soy sauce
2 tablespoons olive oil
4 handfuls of baby spinach, washed

Place the coconut milk in a pan and top up with enough water to cook the rice in. Bring to the boil, add a pinch of salt and the rice. Cook until the rice is tender, then drain in a colander. Pour a little more water into the pan and put it back on the heat. Place the colander over the pan and simmer the water to steam the rice, making it light and fluffy. Place in a warm serving bowl, add the soy sauce and olive oil and stir in the spinach. The heat from the rice will cook the spinach in a matter of minutes, keeping it lovely and green and retaining all its goodness.

vegetables

good old mashed veg

This is a gutsy veg dish which just about everyone loves. My missus makes me fantastic mashed vegetables, beautifully seasoned and drizzled with olive oil – the only thing is, they are meant to be separate servings of boiled carrots and new potatoes! So if you, too, are prone to overcooking your veg, just mash it all together.

serves 4
2kg/4¹/₂lb root vegetables (celeriac, potatoes,
    swede, parsnips, carrots, Jerusalem artichokes)
salt and freshly ground black pepper
extra virgin olive oil or butter

Feel free to use any single vegetable or a mixture of your favourites. Simply peel them, chop them up into golf-ball sized pieces, place in salted boiling water and cook until nice and tender. Drain in a colander before placing the veg back in the pan and mashing with a potato masher. Make it as smooth or as chunky as you like. Season carefully, then enrich the flavour with extra virgin olive oil or butter, or both, to taste.

Once cooked, the mash can be kept warm in a bowl covered with kitchen foil over simmering water. This is handy when cooking for a dinner party, as you can get one lot of veg done and nicely out of the way.

vegetables

baked beetroot with balsamic vinegar, marjoram and garlic

A fantastic veg which is great served with white fish such as grilled monkfish, or with beef carpaccio (see page 175), or as part of an antipasti plate along with some tasty beans, sliced prosciutto and tomato-rubbed crostini. If you're lucky enough to buy beetroots with their leaves, remove them, keep them and use like spinach – they taste amazing.

serves 4
455g/1lb fresh raw beetroots, preferably golf-ball size, scrubbed
10 cloves of garlic, unpeeled and squashed
1 handful of fresh marjoram or sweet oregano, leaves picked
salt and freshly ground black pepper
10 tablespoons balsamic vinegar
6 tablespoons extra virgin olive oil

Preheat the oven to 200°C/400°F/gas 6. Tear off around a metre and a half (5ft) of kitchen foil and fold it in half to give you double thickness. If you can only get larger beetroots halve them to speed up their cooking time, otherwise use them whole. Place them in the middle of the foil with the garlic and marjoram, season generously with salt and freshly ground black pepper, then fold the sides in to the middle. Before you seal the foil, add the vinegar and olive oil. Scrunch or fold the foil together to seal at the top. Place in the preheated oven and cook for around 1 hour, until tender. Serve in the bag at the table – lovely.

baked carrots with cumin, thyme, butter and Chardonnay

I love this dish made with baby carrots, but feel free to use fat old ones sliced at an angle if you please. Butter and wine make a fantastic sauce which just makes it for me. Serve with anything you like.

serves 4
455g/1lb baby carrots, preferably organic, scrubbed and
   left whole
$^1/_2$ teaspoon cumin seeds, crushed
1 handful of fresh thyme leaves
4 knobs of butter
1 glass of Chardonnay
salt and freshly ground black pepper

Preheat the oven to 220°C/425°F/gas 7. Tear off around a metre and a half (5ft) of kitchen foil and fold it in half to give you double thickness. Place everything but the wine and seasoning in the middle of the foil. Bring up the sides and pour in the white wine. Season well. Fold or scrunch the foil together to seal. Cook in the preheated oven for 45 minutes until the carrots are tender. You may need to cook for longer if the carrots are bigger than baby ones.

vegetables

219

bread

basic bread recipe

30g/1oz fresh yeast or 3 x 7g sachets dried yeast
30g/1oz honey (or sugar)
625ml/just over 1 pint tepid water
1kg/just over 2lb strong bread flour
30g/1oz salt
some extra flour for dusting

Stage 1

Dissolve the yeast and honey (or sugar) in half the tepid water.

Stage 2

On a clean surface or in a large bowl, make a pile of the flour and salt. Make a well in the centre and pour in all the dissolved yeast mixture. With 4 fingers of one hand, make circular movements from the centre moving outwards, slowly bringing in more and more of the flour until all the yeast mixture is soaked up. Then pour the other half of the tepid water into the centre and gradually incorporate all the flour to make a moist dough. (Certain flours may need a little more water, so don't be afraid to adjust the quantities.)

Stage 3

Kneading! This is the best bit, just rolling, pushing and folding the dough over and over for 5 minutes. This develops the gluten and the structure of the dough. If any of the dough sticks to your hands, just rub them together with a little extra flour.

Stage 4

Flour both your hands well, and lightly flour the top of the dough. Make it into a roundish shape and place on a baking tray. Deeply score the dough with a knife – allowing it to relax and prove with ease. Leave it to prove until it's doubled in size. Ideally you want a warm, moist, draught-free place for the quickest prove, for example near a warm cooker, in the airing cupboard or just in a warmish room, and you can even cover it with clingfilm if you want to speed things up. This proving process improves the flavour and texture of the dough and should take around 40 minutes, depending on the conditions.

When the dough has doubled in size you need to knock the air out of it by bashing it around for a minute. Now you can shape it into whatever shape is required – round, flat, filled, trayed up, tinned up or whatever – and leave it to prove for a second time until it doubles in size again. The important thing is not to lose your confidence now. Don't feel a need to rush through this, because the second proving time will give you the lovely, delicate soft texture that we all love in fresh bread.

Now it's time to cook your loaf. After all your hard work, don't spoil your efforts. You want to keep all the air inside the loaf, so don't knock it. Gently place it in the preheated oven, don't slam the door. Bake according to the time and temperature given in the recipe variations which follow. You can tell if your bread is cooked by tapping its bottom (if it's in a tin you'll have to take it out). If it sounds hollow it's cooked, if it doesn't then pop it back in for a little longer. Place it on a rack to cool. You're going to love this bread!

chocolate twister bread

1 × basic bread recipe (pages 222–3)
200g/7oz soft butter
200g/7oz hazelnuts, lightly roasted and crushed or broken up
310g/11oz chocolate (70% cocoa), the best you can get,
    smashed up or grated

At Stage 5 of the basic recipe, divide the dough into 2 equal parts. After proving for the second time, take each piece of dough and push out into a squarish shape on a floured board. Then roll out to about 17cm/7 inches wide. At this point, roll the other way and keep rolling to achieve a long rectangle about 0.5cm/$\frac{1}{4}$ inch thick – it doesn't have to be exact. Using a knife, spread the butter thinly across the dough. Sprinkle over the hazelnuts and chocolate and roll up across the width like a Swiss roll. Cut across into 2cm/1 inch wide slices. Place the slices next to each other on a greased baking tray, cut side upwards (rather like Chelsea buns), with small gaps in between. Bake in a preheated oven at 200°C/400°F/gas 6 for around 20 minutes. Allow to cool for 20 minutes before eating with a glass of cold milk.

fruit loaf

Don't worry if you haven't got a tin to make this in. Simply shape into a round, place on a flour-dusted tray and score in a criss-cross fashion.

1 × basic bread recipe (pages 222–3)
a pinch of ground cinnamon
1 clove, ground
200g/7oz dried apricots
100g/3¾oz dried dates
200g/7oz dried raisins

Place the spices and fruit in a food processor or chop very finely. Scrunch into the dough mixture at Stage 2 of the basic recipe, possibly holding back a little water from the recipe as residual water in dried fruit varies. Once you have a good bread consistency, carry on as normal until Stage 5.

After knocking all the air out of the dough, pack it into an appropriately sized greased and floured bread tin. The unproved dough should just underfill the tin, so at the end of Stage 5, when it's proved for the second time, the bread will have doubled in size and will be a whopping great light and fruity blooming bloomer. Lovely. Bake in a preheated oven for around 50 minutes at 200°C/400°F/gas 6, then remove from the tin and put the loaf back in the oven for a final 10 minutes until it sounds hollow when tapped. Allow to cool for 30 minutes.

Gennaro bread

This is a bread very similar to one my mate Gennaro used to make with the leftover, slightly dried-up, unwanted cheese and remaining prosciutto. The bread looks fantastic baked in unglazed, clean little terracotta pots but, quite frankly, you can cook this bread as rolls or as a loaf. Adjust the cooking time accordingly.

1 × basic bread recipe (pages 222–3)
400g/14oz mixed cheese (use Parmesan, fontina, taleggio
    and a little Gorgonzola), grated or broken up
4 large egg yolks
10 slices of prosciutto, torn up
1 handful of fresh basil, torn

At Stage 2 of the basic recipe, mix in all the ingredients and carry on through to Stage 5, when you should divide your bread dough into 6 balls. I like to put them into 6 small, greased and floured, terracotta plant pots. Flour the top and allow to prove until doubled in size. Carefully transfer to the preheated oven and bake for around 30 minutes at 220°C/425°F/gas 7.

pizzas

Pizza bases are great to make as they only need to prove once. The recipe below makes enough for 4 pizza bases. Top with one of my 3 suggested toppings or some of your own favourite ones.

pizza base
1 × basic bread recipe (pages 222–3)

At Stage 5 of the basic recipe, divide your dough into 4 pieces and simply roll each into a large, plate-sized, slightly irregular round shape about 0.5cm/¼ inch thick, using a rolling-pin. Once you've added your chosen topping, place the pizza directly on to the bars of your preheated oven and bake for around 5–7 minutes at 240°C/475°F/gas 9 until the topping has melted and the pizza base is lightly golden.

olive, tomato, rocket, Parmesan and mozzarella pizza

Halve and deseed 8 ripe plum tomatoes and dice them. Place in a bowl with 2 good handfuls of destoned olives. Season with salt and freshly ground black pepper, a touch of olive oil and a splash of red wine vinegar. Smear this on to each pizza base, then sprinkle with pieces of mozzarella. Bake as above, then remove from the oven and sprinkle with some lightly dressed rocket and a good shaving of Parmesan cheese.

mushroom, mozzarella, thyme and spicy sausage meat pizza

Slice up 6 fat field mushrooms and fry with a good handful of fresh thyme and some chopped garlic in a little olive oil until golden. Season well with salt and freshly ground black pepper and remove from the heat. Add a little extra olive oil and smear the mushrooms evenly over each pizza base. Split the skins of 4 spicy sausages and sprinkle very small pieces of the meat on top of the mushrooms. Scatter with a little chopped fresh chilli, add a little mozzarella or other melting cheese – taleggio or fontina – and bake in the oven as above.

mozzarella, prosciutto and basil pizza

Rub your pizza bases with olive oil and randomly scatter with pieces of buffalo mozzarella. Rip over some fresh basil and 2 or 3 nice slices of prosciutto or Parma ham. Bake in the oven as above and serve grated with fresh Parmesan.

chickpea Moroccan flatbread

A very quick bread to make as it only needs one prove. Great for filling with salad, salsas and grilled meats, and especially tasty cooked on barbecues. Also great served with all the tapas recipes (pages 36–51).

1 × basic bread recipe (pages 222–3)
1 tablespoon of cumin seeds, lightly cracked
1 tablespoon of coriander seeds, lightly cracked
1 × 400g tin of chickpeas, drained and mashed

At Stage 2 of the basic recipe, mix in the cumin seeds, coriander seeds and chickpeas and carry on through the recipe as normal until Stage 5, when you should divide your batch of dough into 10 pieces. Roll out each of these to 0.5cm/¼ inch thick and gently pull out into a slightly irregular oval shape. Cook 1 or 2 at a time, depending on how big your oven is, straight away without a second prove, directly on the bars of the preheated oven at 230°C/450°F/gas 8. They take about 4 minutes to cook and puff up beyond belief. Allow to cool slightly for a couple of minutes before eating.

slashed cheese, chilli and paprika flatbread

Great with salads and salamis. Oh, and roast chicken.

1 × basic bread recipe (pages 222–3)
150g/5$\frac{1}{2}$oz goat's cheese, broken up
150g/5$\frac{1}{2}$oz fresh Parmesan cheese, grated
1 heaped tablespoon paprika
4–6 dried red chillies, crumbled

Add all the ingredients at Stage 2 of the basic recipe, then carry on through to Stage 5, when, after knocking out the air, you should divide the bread into 2 pieces and roll them out in an irregular elongated triangle shape, about 1.5cm/$\frac{3}{4}$ inch thick. Slash the bread about 5 or 6 times and stretch it open to expose the gaps. Place on a large baking tray and allow to prove for around 20 minutes before baking in a preheated oven at 220°C/425°F/ gas 7 for 15–20 minutes until golden. Allow to cool for 10 minutes before eating.

desserts

You little tiger. Naughty but nice. I can't, I can't, I can't . . . oooh, go on then. We always try to say no to dessert but, quite frankly, if you want it, have it. I'm sure I'll be quoted on this in ten years' time when I've got a workman's bum and giant lovehandles! Desserts aren't always fattening or unhealthy, but if you feel guilty after eating them then walk up the stairs instead of taking the lift, that's my philosophy. This is a small collection of tasty and very simple desserts – not technical or massively precise, which is the kind of vibe I think most people like at home as opposed to being in my commercial kitchen.

orange and polenta biscuits

Extremely simple and slightly unusual cookie type biscuits, with the polenta giving a fantastic crunch. Great with ice-cream, chocolatey things or simply with a cup of coffee.

makes around 25 biscuits
170g/6oz butter
170g/6oz sugar
255g/9oz polenta
100g/3¾oz plain flour
zest of 2–3 oranges, finely chopped
2 large eggs

Rub the butter, sugar, polenta and flour together before mixing in the orange zest and the eggs. Cover with clingfilm and put in the fridge for an hour until slightly firm. Place a large square of greaseproof paper on a baking tray and spoon small teaspoons of the mixture in lines 5cm/2 inches apart. Bake in a preheated oven at 190°C/375°F/gas 5 for around 5–6 minutes until the outside edges of your biscuits are lightly golden. Remove from the oven and allow to cool for 15 minutes before eating.

chocolate pots

The beauty of this dessert is that it is so smooth, silky and rich. However, if you want to lighten the texture to make it into more of a mousse, then follow the recipe here but fold in 2 stiffly whipped egg whites before pouring into the pots. Small servings are the key – I generally use espresso cups as they're the ideal size. Chocolate pots are brilliant for dinner parties as you can make them up the day before and stick them in the fridge until needed. They are ideal served with the orange and polenta biscuits on page 241.

serves 4
285ml/½ pint single cream
200g/7oz best-quality cooking chocolate (70% cocoa solids)
2 large egg yolks
3 tablespoons brandy, the best you can get
20g/¾oz butter

In a thick-bottomed pan, heat the cream until nearly boiling. Remove and set aside for 1 minute before snapping in your chocolate. Stir in until melted and smooth. Once melted, beat in your egg yolks and brandy and stir until smooth. Allow to cool slightly before stirring in the butter until the mixture is smooth. Pour into individual serving pots.

PS Sometimes if you add the butter when the chocolate isn't cool enough it will make the chocolate look as if it has split. To rectify this, allow the mixture to cool a little longer before whisking in a little cold milk until you have a smooth consistency again.

desserts

two-nuts chocolate torte

This is the best chocolate nut thang around. The day after you should try crumbling it over some ice-cream with a little espresso poured over the top. I always bake this torte in a cheesecake or spring-loaded tin or I make small ones baked in those trays you can use for mince pies, but you can use any well-greased and floured cake tin.

serves 8
150g/5½oz shelled and peeled almonds
150g/5½oz shelled walnuts, finely ground
300g/11oz best-quality cooking chocolate (70% cocoa solids)
1 heaped teaspoon best-quality cocoa powder
255g/9oz butter
100g/3½oz caster sugar
6 large free-range eggs, separated
salt

Preheat the oven to 190°C/375°F/gas 5. Line the bottom of a 20 or 25cm/8- or 10-inch tin with a piece of greaseproof paper before buttering the bottom and sides then dusting with flour. Place the nuts into a food processor and whizz up until finely ground. Then add the chocolate and cocoa and whizz for 30 seconds to break up the chocolate. Put to one side in a separate bowl. Add the butter and sugar to the food processor and beat until pale and fluffy. At this point add the egg yolks one at a time then mix together with the chocolate and nuts.

In another bowl beat the egg whites with a pinch of salt until they form stiff peaks. Gently fold the egg whites into the chocolate, butter and nut mix. Pour all the mixture into the tin. Bake in the preheated oven for around an hour. To test if the torte is cooked, insert a cocktail stick or the tip of a knife for 5 seconds; when removed it should be reasonably clean. Serve with whipped cream, ice-cream or crème fraîche.

a kinda Portuguese custard pie

After eating some fantastic Portuguese cream tarts I was baffled by the crisp, light and almost chewy pastry. I tried to find out the secret to making the pastry but had no luck. So I have come up with a cunning plan to imitate it, which I think is fantastic. I found the filling kinda boring, so I've tweaked it to give it a bit of life. Might look like a palaver but is in fact the quickest custard pie around.

makes around 16 pastry cases

pastry
approx. 255g/9oz slab of puff pastry
1 egg yolk
4 tablespoons caster sugar
a light grating of nutmeg
a couple of pinches of cinnamon

Dust a surface with flour and roll out your pastry to a bit bigger than an A4 size sheet of paper. Brush with the egg yolk and scatter the rest of the ingredients over, being subtle with the nutmeg and cinnamon. Roll the pastry up tightly like a Swiss roll to make a long sausage shape. With a knife, cut across the sausage into 2.5cm/1 inch pieces. Take 8 pieces aside and freeze the rest of the pastry for a rainy day.

Preheat the oven to 200°C/400°F/gas 6. Turn all the pieces of pastry swirl-side up and flatten them slightly. Dust the surface and your pastry with flour, then roll each piece out into a thin circle (around the size of a teacup saucer). Even I don't have proper pastry moulds at home, so I just grease and flour the outsides of 8 of my glass tumblers. Then I place a circle of pastry on top of each tumbler, pleating, pinching and hugging the pastry around them. Place the tumblers on a baking tray, pastry at the top, and put in the preheated oven for around 15 minutes until crisp and golden.

Remove from the oven and, while still hot, take a tea-towel and pat the slightly raised top of the pastry back down on to the flat bottom of the tumbler – giving you a flat base again. Allow to cool and carefully remove the pastry cases from around the tumblers. Fill your pastry cases with the custard filling (page 248).

makes enough to fill 8 pastry cases

custard
6 large organic eggs
4 dessertspoons good runny honey
2 vanilla pods, scored lengthwise and seeds removed
zest of 1 orange
565ml/1 pint double cream

Whip up the eggs, honey, vanilla seeds and orange zest in a bowl. (Don't waste the vanilla pods; simply pop them in a jar with some sugar to make a tasty vanilla sugar.) At the same time, in a thick-bottomed pan, heat the cream until nearly boiling. Add it immediately to the rest of the ingredients in the bowl, while whipping fast with a whisk for 30 seconds. Add the mixture back to the pan on a medium heat, stirring continuously and using a spatula to get into the edges. This is a very quick and almost aggressive method of cooking a thick egg custard – which is normally done in a bowl over simmering water or in the oven in a bain-marie, like a brûlée – so keep stirring to keep your custard smooth. When it gets as thick as thick yoghurt, spoon it into your pastry cases and allow to cool. A skin will begin to form on the top of each pie. To finish them off, make a little caramel . . .

caramel
1 big handful of caster sugar
3 tablespoons of water

Place the sugar and water in a pan. Bring to the boil and gently agitate until golden brown. At this point it will be hotter than hot – *don't even think about tasting it*. No kids allowed. Dribble the mixture randomly over your custard tarts – it will bubble and cool to a crisp caramel. Fantastic. Oh yeah – place the pan in the sink and half fill with water before boiling it up again – you'll have no grief washing it up.

crème brûlée the way I like it

I have eaten crème brûlées all over the gaff and, at the end of the day, an egg custard is an egg custard. Some are good and some are overcooked and bad, but the most important thing is that the custard should only be an inch thick, with a lovely crisp layer of thin caramel on top. So many people plonk their custard mix into a deep ramekin dish with a fat layer of hard caramel on top and that's just not right.

serves 6
300g/11oz fresh rhubarb
3 tablespoons caster sugar
2 vanilla pods
300ml/11fl oz double cream
200ml/7fl oz full fat milk
8 egg yolks
80g/2¾oz sugar

Preheat the oven to 140°C/275°F/gas 1. Roughly slice up the rhubarb and place it in a pan with the caster sugar and 5 tablespoons of water. Simmer until tender, divide between 6 small serving dishes which your brûlée will be cooked in, then set aside.

Score the vanilla pods lengthwise and run the knife up the pod to remove the vanilla seeds. Scrape these into the pan with the pods, cream and milk and slowly bring to the boil. Meanwhile beat together the yolks and the sugar in a bowl until light and fluffy. When the cream and milk are just boiling, remove the vanilla pods and add little by little to the egg mixture, whisking continuously. I like to remove any bubbles or froth from the mixture before dividing it into the serving dishes, on top of the rhubarb. Stand these in an appropriately sized roasting tray filled with water half-way up the containers, and bake in the preheated oven for around 25 minutes until the custard mixture has set but is still slightly wobbly in the centre.

Allow to cool to room temperature then place in the fridge until ready to serve. Sprinkle with sugar and caramelize under a very hot grill or using a kitchen blowtorch. Lovely.

Sheila's pudding

This is a variation of the classic Eve's pudding which uses stewed apples. I love peaches for this pudding, though many fruits can be used, such as rhubarb with almonds or plums on their own. I called it Sheila's pudding for a laugh really . . . I'm a strange boy.

serves 6
6 ripe peaches or nectarines, halved and stones removed
4 heaped teaspoons demerara sugar
1 vanilla pod, scored lengthwise and seeds removed
125g/4½oz butter
125g/4½oz caster sugar
2 large free-range eggs
125g/4½oz self-raising flour

Preheat the oven to 180°C/350°F/gas 4. Put the peaches in a saucepan with the demerara sugar, the vanilla seeds and 4 tablespoons of water. Simmer for 5 minutes and then place into a well-greased and lightly floured ovenproof dish or bowl. Beat together the butter, caster sugar and eggs until light and fluffy. Add the flour, mix thoroughly and spread over the peaches.

Bake in the preheated oven for 45 minutes. Remove from the oven and serve with hot custard or something cold, like vanilla ice-cream or crème fraîche.

party cake

3 rounded tablespoons cocoa powder
200g/7oz caster sugar
200g/7oz butter
3 large eggs, preferably free-range
200g/7oz self-raising flour, sifted
1 rounded teaspoon baking powder
1 handful of flaked almonds
200ml/7fl oz double cream

1 large handful of raspberries
1 large handful of strawberries

chocolate topping
100g/3¾oz butter
100g/3¾oz best cooking chocolate
100g/3¾oz icing sugar
3 tablespoons milk

Preheat the oven to 180°C/350°F/gas 4. Line the bases of 2 x 20cm/8-inch cake tins with greased greaseproof paper. Mix the cocoa powder with 4 tablespoons of boiling water until smooth. In a separate bowl, beat the sugar and butter until fluffy, add the cocoa mixture, eggs, flour and baking powder. Mix well, fold in the nuts. Divide the mixture between the tins. Bake for about 25 minutes. When cooked, allow to cool then remove from the tins.

Melt the chocolate topping ingredients in a bowl over some lightly simmering water. Stir until blended well and allow to cool. Whip the double cream to soft peaks and sweeten with a little sugar to taste. To assemble the cake, remove the greaseproof paper from both sponges. Drizzle each one with a little sherry if you like. Spread the cream over one of the sponges, then sprinkle the fruit on top. Sandwich the second sponge on top and press down. Run a knife around the edge of the cake to smooth it off and drizzle over your chocolate topping. Happy days, you've done it! But allow the chocolate topping to firm up slightly before tucking in.

paros

strawberries marinated in balsamic vinegar

serves 4
2–3 big punnets of strawberries
approx. 5 tablespoons sugar, to taste
10 tablespoons balsamic vinegar
1 vanilla pod, scored lengthwise and seeds removed
400g/14oz mascarpone cheese
4 or 5 leaves of fresh mint or basil, finely sliced

When the strawberries taste pukka and are juicy like they should be, pinch off the stalks, place in a bowl and scatter generously with the sugar followed by the balsamic vinegar. Stir around and allow to marinate for up to 2 hours. Mix the vanilla seeds with the mascarpone cheese and sweeten to taste with a little sugar. Don't forget you can use the vanilla pod to flavour a small jar of sugar. Place a big lob of mascarpone on a plate covered with a generous heap of strawberries and the tasty balsamic juice. A fine scattering of mint or basil will freshen it slightly.

   PS If you find you have any leftover strawberries and marinade, squash it all up, freeze for 2½ hours and you've got a lovely frappé (see page 261).

Maltesers and ice-cream

serves 4
2 packets of Maltesers
a tub of good vanilla ice-cream

Bash Maltesers and sprinkle over a generous serving of vanilla ice-cream.

Campari and passionfruit sorbet

serves 4
285ml/½ pint water
200g/7oz sugar
15 passionfruit
1 wine glass of Campari

Place the water and sugar in a pan, bring to the boil and simmer for 5 minutes. Remove from the heat and allow to cool for a while. Halve your passionfruit and scoop out the flesh, seeds and juice using a spoon. Stir this up – you can pass it through a coarse sieve to remove the seeds, but quite frankly I think that's a palaver. I like the seeds. Mix the passionfruit with the Campari and sugar syrup in a plastic tub or earthenware dish and place in the freezer. Generally, sorbet takes 2 hours to set. Try to stir it around every half an hour if you remember. Serve on its own, with some seasonal fruit, or in a cone with some vanilla ice-cream.

pineapple and grapefruit frappé

This recipe works with just about any fruit or combination of your choice because the principle is so basic. A frappé is basically a cross between a granita (like an icy Slush Puppy) and a smooth sorbet. As both pineapples and grapefruits can vary so much in natural sweetness, add the sugar to your own taste.

serves 4
2 ripe pineapples, peeled and roughly chopped
3 grapefruits, halved and juiced
sugar to taste

Whizz up the pineapple in a liquidizer until smooth and pass through a coarse sieve. Add the grapefruit juice and stir in sugar to taste, remembering that the sweetness from the sugar will lessen slightly when frozen, so use a touch more than you normally would. Place in the freezer for around 2½ hours to set, stirring every 45 minutes.

ben

When I first moved to London in 1992 all I heard with regard to cocktails and fine drinks was 'Dick Bradsell this', 'Dick Bradsell that'. His name cropped up so often I thought he was a film star. Having trained at Zanzibar in London, his precision and natural flair for mixing cocktails, and his obvious ability to evolve his drinks in new ventures, led to him setting up many great cocktail bars. With his name behind Dick's Bar at the Atlantic in Piccadilly, he also set up bars at the Soho Brasserie, the Moscow Club, the Café de Paris, Fred's Club, the Player, the Flamingo, and, most recently, Match Bar.

It wasn't until five years later that I had the pleasure of meeting him at the Player – he shook my hand and gave me one of the most memorable drinks I'd ever drunk. It sounds over the top from someone who knows nothing about cocktails, but it was bloomin' fantastic. He spoke to me for five minutes. In that time he made me realize that cocktail-making is no different from cooking. When I say this, what I mean is that sometimes there are measurements and guidelines but a lot of the time it is open to innovation and natural flair. I was blown away by the way he described making drinks – his eyes lit up and his animated body language said it all to me. Passion.

I hadn't spoken to Dick again until I was thinking about having this bevvies section in my book. Personally, I thought he was the only person for the job and I knew he'd do us all proud. So we sat down together and have come up with a whole range of drinks for you that can easily be made at home. All of the spirits and liqueurs mentioned can be bought from any good off-licence or at a reasonable price, mail order, from *Class* magazine (Freephone 0808 1002691), where you can also buy cocktail-making starter kits and accessories.

dick

dry Martini

There are so many different ways of making this and, just for us, Dick has come up with a 'naked' Martini in the 'Franklin Style', which means it's poured straight from the freezer without being stirred over ice in the traditional way. It's named after Franklin D. Roosevelt, who preferred to have 2 olives in his.

naked
Take a frozen cocktail glass from the freezer, put a couple of drops of dry vermouth into the glass and top with freezing cold vodka or gin. Add 2 olives.

stirred
Fill a jug with ice, splash on some vermouth, stir and then discard the liquid. Your ice is now coated in vermouth. Add 75ml of gin or vodka to this and stir as many times as you like. Strain into a pre-chilled glass before garnishing with an olive or a slice of lemon.

shaken
You can shake a Martini but the result will be a cloudy drink with little bits of broken ice on top. The cocktail of choice for James Bond, of course.

Tom Collins

The original Tom Collins employed sweet Old Tom gin, but unfortunately this is now only available in the Far East. If using London dry gin the drink is a John Collins. The vodka version is conveniently known as a Vodka Collins. Shaking a Collins and pouring it neat into a glass then adding soda water creates a Gin Fizz. And a Sling was originally the basic Collins recipe made with plain water – definitely one of the earliest of cocktails. To make the sugar syrup, mix an equal amount of sugar and boiling water together and stir until clear. Or you can buy it from any good off-licence.

Into a shaker pour 50ml of gin, 40ml of fresh lemon juice and 3 teaspoons of sugar syrup. Shake with ice and then strain over fresh ice in a tumbler. Fill to the top with soda water and stir. Garnish with a lemon slice and a cherry.

old fashioned

This is a drink for purists. It needs a very good-quality spirit, so Dick suggests using Wild Turkey or Maker's Mark bourbon, Cockspur, Mountgay or Myers rum and any decent brandy. The idea is to take a dark spirit like brandy, bourbon or rum and bring out its natural depth of flavour; you sweeten it then give it depth by adding bitters. Perform the same ritual each time you make this and you'll get it right every time.

Take an old-fashioned glass like a whisky tumbler and pour in 4 drops of bitters and 2 teaspoons of sugar syrup (although this depends on the sweetness of your chosen spirit – brandy needs more, rum needs less). See the Tom Collins recipe on page 266 for a note about making sugar syrup. Then add 2 ice cubes and stir. Add 2 more ice cubes, 25ml of your preferred spirit and stir. Then 2 more ice cubes and a further 25ml of your spirit. Stir. Then more ice and stir again. The 50ml of alcohol should now fill your glass as the ice has diluted it. Garnish with a twist of orange or lemon – lemon being particularly good with rum.

Bellini

This is the famous drink from Harry's Bar in Venice, where they have a monopoly on the best peaches in the world. Over there they use the local Italian sparkling wine called prosecco. The drink tastes far better when you use this fizz, so try to get hold of some. Rather than being served in a champagne glass, the original was served in a small tumbler, but you can use either.

Use fresh peach purée if you wish. Alternatively, take a peach, blanch it in hot water to remove the skin, stone it, then blend it with a little dash of prosecco. Fill one third of your glass with the peach purée and top *carefully* with prosecco as it will fizz up manically. Stir as you are pouring, to fill the glass.

The junior version of this is a Virgin Bellini, where you replace the prosecco with soda. Often a dash of sugar helps.

caipirinha

This is a traditional Brazilian drink made with the local spirit, cachaça, and the local citrus fruit, limon (little green limes with seeds). There are many different ways of making this drink – this version is the way Dick was taught to make it by an eccentric Brazilian gentleman. To replicate the flavour of hard-to-find cachaça, use almost 2 shots (50ml) of light rum and a splash of tequila.

You will need to crush some ice first. You can do this by placing it in a bag, covering it with a tea-towel and bashing it with a rolling-pin, as you would if you were making a crumble base out of biscuits. Take a lime, chop the ends off it and cut it into about 16 small pieces. Put in a glass tumbler, coat with about 2 teaspoons of sugar syrup (see page 266) and crush the limes to release their oils into the sugar. People often use brown sugar or white sugar in the belief that this accelerates the releasing of the oils, so experiment. You can use the rolling-pin to do this, but be careful, as you are using pressure in a glass. Fill the glass with crushed ice and add 50ml of cachaça. Stir and drink!

daiquiri natural

This drink must be made to the exact recipe measurements, as you are playing with the sourness of lime set against the sweetness of rum and if you don't get it exact the resulting imbalance in the flavour will be very obvious. The ratio is 8 parts rum to 2 parts lime and will only work with the correct rum, although other rums will have to do if you cannot find Havana Club.

For one drink, pour 50ml of Havana Club rum, 12.5ml of freshly squeezed lime juice and 1 teaspoon of sugar syrup (see page 266) into a shaker. Add lightly cracked ice cubes and shake thoroughly until the shaker becomes frosted, then strain through a mesh, such as a tea-strainer, into a pre-chilled cocktail glass.

mojito

This is Dick's favourite summer drink for when he's relaxing in his hammock. You can make this with vodka or tequila, or even cachaça if you want, but for the true Cuban feel you do need Cuban rum. Place 3–5 small mint leaves in a glass. Coat with 2–3 teaspoons of sugar syrup (see page 266) and crush to release the mint oil. Add the juice of 1 fresh lime and 50ml of Havana Club rum. Fill the glass with crushed or cracked ice. You can add a little soda if you wish. Stir thoroughly before drinking.

watermelon vodka

This is a really funny thing that I saw an American friend of mine make. Great for a barbie or party. Wish I'd known about this when I was going to school parties – I could have walked in with my watermelon and got all my mates completely sloshed! Needs to be started three days – even a week – before you plan to eat it.

1 large, ripe watermelon – give it a smell and
    a slap to check for ripeness
1 bottle of best vodka (or even champagne)

Simply cut a hole in the top of the melon, wide and deep enough to insert a funnel. Make sure the funnel fits quite tightly or the liquid will spill out. If that happens cut a larger hole. Pour some of your chosen alcohol into the melon through the funnel, leave to sit for a day and pour in some more. The flesh will absorb the liquid, so pour in some more the next day – basically until it becomes saturated. When ready to serve, slice up into nice big pieces and get all your mates plastered on it!

frothy Malteser milk

1 packet of Maltesers
285ml/½ pint cold milk

In a liquidizer or food processor, whizz up the
Maltesers to a powder and add the milk until frothy.

smoothies

I love smoothies, because you can make them with anything you like. Here's a basic smoothie recipe which you can flavour with 2–3 handfuls of any chosen fruit. Or flavour it using one of the three fantastic combinations given below.

for 2 people
1 banana
2–3 large handfuls of your chosen fruit
approx 1 pint glass of ice
285ml/½ pint single cream

Place the banana and your chosen fruit into a liquidizer and whizz for 30 seconds. Add the ice and cream. Place the lid back on tightly and pulse the liquidizer a couple of times on and off to break up the larger pieces of ice, before whizzing up to a semi-slushy milkshake consistency.

   If you haven't got a liquidizer, you can do as I have been known to do – place the ice into a clean tea-towel and bash the hell out of it with a rolling-pin before stirring in the mushed fruit and the cream. It's good, but not quite as good. The 3 smoothies below can be made by following this basic recipe, using the listed ingredients as your chosen fruit.

blackberry and pineapple smoothie

2 handfuls of blackberries
1 handful of peeled and chopped fresh pineapple

banana and honey smoothie

1 more banana
2 tablespoons honey
2 heaped tablespoons peanut butter (if you're very sad)

raspberry and strawberry smoothie

1 handful of raspberries
2 handfuls of strawberries

stocks, sauces,
bits, bobs, this,
that and the other

chicken stock

for 4 litres/7 pints of stock
2kg/4½lb raw chicken carcasses, chopped
½ a head of garlic, broken up but unpeeled
6 handfuls of fragrant root vegetables (celery, onions, carrots), chopped
3 bay leaves
3 handfuls of mixed fresh herbs (rosemary, parsley, thyme)
5 whole black peppercorns
5 litres/8¾ pints cold water

Chuck all the ingredients into a large, deep pan and bring to the boil. Turn the heat down and simmer for 1–3 hours, skimming as necessary. Pass through a sieve, and once cool you can keep it in the fridge for 4 days or the freezer for up to 3 months.

fish stock

for 3 litres/5 pints of stock
6 handfuls of fragrant root vegetables (celery, fennel, onion), chopped
½ a head of garlic, broken up and sliced thinly
2 dried red chillies
2kg/4½lb fish bones, chopped and washed thoroughly
2 tablespoons olive oil
255ml/9fl oz white wine
3.5 litres/6 pints cold water
6 sprigs of fresh parsley
1 sprig of fresh thyme

In a large, deep pan, slowly fry the vegetables, garlic, chillies and fish bones in olive oil until the vegetables are tender. Add the white wine and cook for another 2 or 3 minutes. Add the water and bring to the boil. Simmer for 20 minutes only, adding all the fresh herbs, and skim regularly. Pass through a sieve and allow to cool. Fish stock can be boiled and reduced to intensify its flavour. It can be stored in the fridge for about 2–3 days, or you can freeze it for 1–2 months. A sign of a good stock is when it's tasty, clear and, when cold, sets like jelly.

stocks, sauces, bits, bobs, this, that and the other

vegetable stock

Half fill your largest deep pan with roughly chopped fragrant vegetables such as celery, fennel, carrots, onions and leeks, and add plum tomatoes and garlic, and herbs and spices such as thyme, rosemary, bay, parsley and chilli. If you have any dried mushrooms add them too, as they give an amazing flavour. Cover with cold water, bring to the boil, and then simmer for 1–2 hours with a lid on the pan. Vegetable stock will keep in the fridge for a week and in the freezer for 2–3 months.

garlic aïoli

serves 8
1 clove of garlic, peeled
1 teaspoon salt
1 large egg yolk
1 teaspoon Dijon mustard
approx. 285ml/½ pint extra virgin olive oil
approx. 285ml/½ pint olive oil
lemon juice, to taste
salt and freshly ground black pepper

Smash up or finely chop the garlic and mix with the salt. Whisk the egg yolk and mustard together in a bowl then slowly start to add the olive oil bit by bit – using two different types will give the aïoli a flavour which isn't too strong or too peppery. Once you've blended in a quarter of the olive oil, start to add the rest in larger amounts. Then add the garlic and lemon juice, along with any optional extra flavours such as basil, fennel tops or dill. Season to taste, adding a little extra juice to taste.

tomato salsa

A really fantastic salsa which is brilliant served with tuna or swordfish. You can remove the skin of the tomatoes if you wish – I quite like the skin left on for this one.

serves 4–6

2 good handfuls of really ripe plum tomatoes, deseeded and finely chopped

1 good handful of small capers, soaked and drained

2 small shallots or 1/2 a red onion, finely chopped

1/2 a clove of garlic, finely chopped

1 good handful of parsley, finely chopped

a couple of swigs of balsamic vinegar, to taste

6–8 lugs of olive oil

dried chilli flakes, to taste

4 anchovy fillets, finely chopped

1/2 a cucumber, peeled, deseeded and finely diced

salt and freshly ground black pepper, to taste

Mix all the ingredients together, season to taste, and you have a brilliant salsa.

salsa verde

The secret of a good salsa verde is to chop all the ingredients very finely and to use it the same day, as it doesn't tend to keep for long, even in the fridge. A fantastic accompaniment to any grilled meat or fish. Particularly good with the sea bass recipe on page 156.

serves 8

2 cloves of garlic, peeled

1 small handful of capers

1 small handful of pickled gherkins (the ones in sweet vinegar)

6 anchovy fillets

2 large handfuls of flat-leaf parsley, leaves picked

1 bunch of fresh basil, leaves picked

1 handful of fresh mint, leaves picked

1 tablespoon Dijon mustard

3 tablespoons red wine vinegar

approx. 120ml/8 tablespoons of your best olive oil

sea salt and freshly ground black pepper

Finely chop the first seven ingredients and put them into a bowl. Add the mustard and red wine vinegar then slowly stir in the olive oil. Balance the flavours with freshly ground black pepper and, if necessary, sea salt and a little more red wine vinegar.

minted bread sauce

serves 4
3 handfuls of fresh mint
1 handful of chopped bread
extra virgin olive oil
salt and freshly ground black pepper
2 teaspoons mustard
red wine vinegar

Finely chop 3 parts mint to 1 part bread and stir in some olive oil until the mix has 'loosened'. Then balance the flavours by carefully seasoning, adding the mustard and splashing in some vinegar to taste. The flavour improves with time.

creamed horseradish

One of the most amazing sauces, this can turn round a simple piece of grilled or roasted beef or a roasted beetroot or carrot. Using the jarred stuff in this recipe can be delicious, but the fresh stuff is a million miles superior. If using fresh horseradish, which can be obtained from bigger supermarkets, peel and grate it.

Whether using jarred or fresh horseradish, put it in a bowl, adding crème frâiche to thin the sauce and mellow the flavour to your taste – in my case, hot. Season carefully with sea salt and freshly ground black pepper and a good splash of white wine vinegar.

index

Page numbers in bold denote illustrations
v indicates vegetarian recipe

a

v   aïoli 276
v   almonds: pan-toasted almonds with a touch of chilli and
       sea salt 39, **39**
     anchovies
       black olive tapenade 42
       farfalle with broccoli, anchovies and chilli 131
       linguine puttanesca 130
       marinated anchovies 48
       spaghetti with anchovies, dried chilli and pangritata
          126, **127**
     artichokes
v   baked Jerusalem artichokes, breadcrumbs, thyme and
          lemon 208, **209**
v   potato and Jerusalem artichoke soup with thyme,
          mascarpone and hazelnuts 85
       warm salad of winter leaves, bacon and Jerusalem
          artichokes **62**, 63
     Asian infused tuna **50**, 51
v   Asian marinade 194, **194**
v   asparagus: ravioli of minted asparagus with potatoes and
       mascarpone 114, **115**
     aubergines
v   blackened sweet aubergines 42
v   stracci, spicy aubergines, tomatoes, basil and
          Parmesan **102**, 103
     avocados
       Asian infused tuna **50**, 51
v   salad of boiled potatoes, avocado and cress **70**, 71

b

     bacon
       risotto of radicchio, smoky bacon, rosemary and red
          wine 144, **145**
       roasted Hamilton poussin wrapped with streaky bacon
          and stuffed with potatoes and sage **182**, 183
       sarnie 24, 25
       warm salad of winter leaves, bacon and Jerusalem
          artichokes **62**, 63
v   baked beetroot with balsamic vinegar, marjoram and
       garlic 216, **217**
v   baked carrots with cumin, thyme, butter and Chardonnay
       218, 219
v   baked endive with thyme, orange juice, garlic and butter
       201
v   baked fennel with garlic butter and vermouth 202, **203**
v   baked Jerusalem artichokes, breadcrumbs, thyme and
       lemon 208, **209**
     baked trout and potatoes with a crème fraîche, walnut
       and horseradish sauce 162, 163
     balsamic vinegar
v   baked beetroot with balsamic vinegar, marjoram and
          garlic 216, **217**
v   basil, balsamic vinegar and pine nut dressing 80
v   spaghetti with red onions, sun-dried tomatoes,
          balsamic vinegar and basil 125
v   strawberries marinated in balsamic vinegar 256, **257**
     banana and honey smoothie 272, **273**

     basil
v   basil, balsamic vinegar and pine nut dressing 80
       beef tomatoes, basil, ham and mild cheese on thick
          toast 30, **31**
       prawn and pea risotto with basil and mint 142, **143**
v   spaghetti with red onions, sun-dried tomatoes,
          balsamic vinegar and basil 125
v   stracci, spicy aubergines, tomatoes, basil and
          Parmesan **102**, 103
     beans
       grilled swordfish, green beans and spicy tomato salsa
          164, **165**
       salad of marinated charred squid with cannellini beans,
          rocket and chilli 74, **75**
       seared scallops and crispy prosciutto with roasted
          tomatoes and smashed white beans 160, **161**
       tray-baked cod with runner beans, pancetta and pine
          nuts 150, **151**
     beef
       Botham burger 196, **197**
       Mary's Saturday soup and dumplings 86, **87**
       roasted fillet of beef rolled in herbs and porcini and
          wrapped in prosciutto 186, **187**
       seared carpaccio of beef with chilli, ginger, radish and
          soy **178**, 179
       seared carpaccio of beef with roasted baby beets,
          creamed horseradish, watercress and Parmesan
          176, **177**
       seared encrusted carpaccio of beef 175
     beef tomatoes, basil, ham and mild cheese on thick toast
       30, **31**
     beetroot
v   baked beetroot with balsamic vinegar, marjoram and
          garlic 216, **217**
       seared carpaccio of beef with roasted baby beets,
          creamed horseradish, watercress and Parmesan
          176, **177**
     Bellini 267
v   biscuits, orange and polenta 240, **241**
v   black olive tapenade 42
     blackberry and pineapple smoothie 272, **273**
v   blackened marinated peppers 45
v   blackened sweet aubergine 42
     Botham burger 196, **197**
     braised five hour lamb with wine, veg and all that 174
     braised pigeon breasts with peas, lettuce and spring
       onions **188**, 189
     bread
v   basic recipe 222–3
v   chickpea Moroccan flatbread **234**, 235
v   chocolate twister bread 226, **227**
v   fruit loaf 228, **229**
       Gennaro bread **230**, 231
       pizzas 232, **233**
v   slashed cheese, chilli and paprika flatbread 236, **237**
v   bread sauce, minted 278
     breakfast
       bacon sarnie 24, 25
       beef tomatoes, basil, ham and mild cheese on thick
          toast 30, **31**
v   figs, honey and ricotta 28, **29**
v   homemade yoghurt 34, 35

midnight pan-cooked breakfast **26**, 27
v Pukkolla 32–3, **33**
bream: wok-fried crispy bream with steamed greens and
    Thai dressing **166**, 167
broccoli: farfalle with broccoli, anchovies and chilli 131
broths *see* soups
burger, Botham **196**, **197**

c
cabbage: farfalle with Savoy cabbage, pancetta, thyme
    and mozzarella **132**, 133
caipirinha 268
Cajun spicy rub 195, **195**
v cake, party 254, **255**
v Campari and passionfruit sorbet **260**, 261
cannellini beans: salad of marinated charred squid with
    cannellini beans, rocket and chilli 74, **75**
v carrots: baked carrots with cumin, thyme, butter and
    Chardonnay **218**, 219
v celeriac: celery, celeriac, parsley and pomegranate salad
    76, 77
v celery, celeriac, parsley and pomegranate salad **76**, 77
cheese
    beef tomatoes, basil, ham and mild cheese on thick
        toast 30, **31**
    Gennaro bread 230, **231**
v   paneer Indian cheese 190
v   slashed cheese, chilli and paprika flatbread 236, **237**
cherry tomatoes
v   squashed cherry tomato and smashed olive salad
        58–9, **58–9**
v   sweet cherry tomato dressing 81
chicken
    fantastic roasted chicken 184, **185**
    I-Thai fried tortellini of chicken, ginger, water chestnut
        and lemon grass with dipping sauce 122–3, **122–3**
    roasted Hamilton poussin wrapped with streaky bacon
        and stuffed with potatoes and sage **182**, 183
    stock 275
chickpeas
    marinated squid with chickpeas and chilli 49
v   chickpea Moroccan flatbread **234**, 235
v   smashed spiced chickpeas 40, **41**
chilli(es)
    farfalle with broccoli, anchovies and chilli 131
    linguine with pancetta, olive oil, chilli, clams and white
        wine 128, **129**
    marinated squid with chickpeas and chilli 49
    monkfish wrapped in banana leaves with ginger,
        coriander, chilli and coconut milk **148**, 149
v   mozzarella and grilled chilli salad 56, **57**
v   pan-toasted almonds with a touch of chilli and sea salt
        39, **39**
    salad of marinated charred squid with cannellini beans,
        rocket and chilli 74, **75**
    seared carpaccio of beef with chilli, ginger, radish and
        soy **178**, 179
v   slashed cheese, chilli and paprika flatbread 236, **237**
    slow-cooked and stuffed baby bell chilli peppers 46,
        47
    spaghetti with anchovies, dried chilli and pangritata
        126, **127**
v   spaghetti with olive oil, garlic, chilli and parsley 125
Chinese greens: wok-fried crispy bream with steamed
    greens and Thai dressing **166**, 167
chocolate
v   chocolate pots 242, **243**
v   chocolate twister bread 226, **227**
v   party cake 254, **255**
v   two-nuts chocolate torte **244**, 245

clams: linguine with pancetta, olive oil, chilli, clams and
    white wine 128, **129**
cocktails
    Bellini 267
    caipirinha 268
    daiquiri natural 269
    dry Martini 266
    mojito 269
    old fashioned 266
    Tom Collins 266
coconut milk
    monkfish wrapped in banana leaves with ginger,
        coriander, chilli and coconut milk **148**, 149
v   steamed spinach with coconut rice 212
cod: tray-baked cod with runner beans, pancetta and pine
    nuts 150, **151**
coriander
v   coriander and crème fraîche dressing 80
    monkfish wrapped in banana leaves with ginger,
        coriander, chilli and coconut milk **148**, 149
v courgettes: smashed courgette paste 43
v couscous with grilled summer vegetables and loadsa
    herbs 60, **61**
cream
    pappardelle with rabbit, herbs and cream 105
    tagliatelle with saffron, seafood and cream 108, **109**
v creamed horseradish 278
v crème brûlée the way I like it **250**, 251
crème fraîche
    baked trout and potatoes with a crème fraîche, walnut
        and horseradish sauce 162, **163**
v   coriander and crème fraîche dressing 80
v cress: salad of boiled potatoes, avocado and cress 70, **71**
v crunchy Thai salad 67, **67**
v cumin: baked carrots with cumin, thyme, butter and
    Chardonnay **218**, 219
curry: Peter's lamb curry 190, **191**
v custard pie, Portuguese 246–9, **246**, **249**

d
daiquiri natural 269
desserts
v   Campari and passionfruit sorbet **260**, 261
v   chocolate pots 242, **243**
v   crème brûlée the way I like it **250**, 251
v   Maltesers and ice-cream 258, **258**
v   orange and polenta biscuits **240**, 241
v   party cake 254, **255**
v   pineapple and grapefruit frappé 261
v   Portuguese custard pie 247–8, **249**
v   Sheila's pudding 252, **253**
v   strawberries marinated in balsamic vinegar 256, **257**
v   two-nuts chocolate torte **244**, 245
dressings
v   basil, balsamic vinegar and pine nut 80
v   coriander and crème fraîche 80
v   mustard and herb vinegar 81
v   olive oil and lemon juice 81
v   sweet cherry tomato 81
v   Thai 80
drinks
    frothy Malteser milk 271, **271**
    smoothies 272, **273**
    watermelon vodka 270, **270**
    see also cocktails
dry Martini 266

e
v endive: baked endive with thyme, orange juice, garlic and
    butter 201

f

farfalle
    with broccoli, anchovies and chilli 131
    with Savoy cabbage, pancetta, thyme and mozzarella
      132, **133**
v fennel: baked fennel with garlic butter and vermouth 202,
    203
v fennel seed, thyme and garlic rub 195, **195**
v figs, honey and ricotta 28, **29**
fish
    pie **158**, 159
    stock 275
    see also individual names
fragrant Thai broth **92**, 93
frothy Malteser milk 271, **271**
v fruit loaf 228, **229**

g

garlic
v aïoli 276
v baked beetroot with balsamic vinegar, marjoram and
    garlic 216, **217**
v baked endive with thyme, orange juice, garlic and
    butter 201
v baked fennel with garlic butter and vermouth 202,
    203
v fennel seed, thyme and garlic rub 195, **195**
v roasted sweet garlic, thyme and mascarpone risotto
    with toasted almonds and breadcrumbs **136**, 137
v rosemary, garlic and lemon marinade 194, **194**
v spaghetti with olive oil, garlic, chilli and parsley 125
v spaghetti with squashed olives, tomatoes, garlic, olive
    oil and chopped rocket 124
v tray-baked field mushrooms studded with garlic
    and rubbed with butter and pounded thyme **204**,
    205
Gennaro bread 230, 231
ginger
    I-Thai fried tortellini of chicken, ginger, water chestnut
      and lemon grass with dipping sauce 122–3, **122–3**
    monkfish wrapped in banana leaves with ginger,
      coriander, chilli and coconut milk **148**, 149
    seared carpaccio of beef with chilli, ginger, radish and
      soy **178**, 179
goat's cheese: white risotto with lemon thyme, sliced
    prosciutto, pecorino and crumbled goat's cheese
    138, **139**
v Gorgonzola: stracci with Gorgonzola, mascarpone,
    marjoram and walnuts 104
v grapefruit: pineapple and grapefruit frappé 261
green beans: grilled swordfish, green beans and spicy
    tomato salsa 164, **165**
grilled butterflied sardines 48
grilled swordfish, green beans and spicy tomato salsa
    164, **165**

h

ham: beef tomatoes, basil, ham and mild cheese on thick
    toast 30, **31**
herbs 16–19
v couscous with grilled summer vegetables and loadsa
    herbs 60, **61**
    pappardelle with rabbit, herbs and cream 105
v ravioli of creamed ricotta, toasted pine nuts, Parmesan
    and loadsa herbs 116
    roasted fillet of beef rolled in herbs and porcini and
      wrapped in prosciutto 186, **187**
    roasted slashed fillet of sea bass stuffed with herbs,
      baked on mushroom potatoes with salsa verde –
      à la Tony Blair 156, **157**

    salmon fillet wrapped in prosciutto with herby lentils,
      spinach and yoghurt 168, **169**
    sea bass baked in a bag and stuffed with herbs 152,
      153
    seafood broth, ripped herbs, toasted bread and garlic
      aïoli 90, **91**
honey
    banana and honey smoothie 272, **273**
v figs, honey and ricotta 28, **29**
horseradish
    baked trout and potatoes with a crème fraîche, walnut
      and horseradish sauce **162**, 163
v creamed horseradish 278
    seared carpaccio of beef with roasted baby beets,
      creamed horseradish, watercress and Parmesan
      176, **177**
v hot and fragrant rub 195, **195**

i

v ice-cream: Maltesers and ice-cream 258, **258**
I-Thai fried tortellini of chicken, ginger, water chestnut
    and lemon grass with dipping sauce 122–3, **122–3**

j

Jerusalem artichokes *see* artichokes

l

lamb
    braised five hour lamb with wine, veg and all that
      174
    Mary's Saturday soup and dumplings 86, **87**
    Peter's lamb curry 190, **191**
lemon(s)
v baked Jerusalem artichokes, breadcrumbs, thyme and
    lemon 208, **209**
v rosemary, garlic and lemon marinade 194, **194**
v spinach and porcini with rosemary and lemon 211
v tortellini of ricotta, lemon, Parmesan and sage butter
    120, **121**
    lemon grass: I-Thai fried tortellini of chicken, ginger,
      water chestnut and lemon grass with dipping sauce
      122–3, **122–3**
    lemon thyme: white risotto with lemon thyme, sliced
      prosciutto, pecorino and crumbled goat's cheese
      138, **139**
    lentils: salmon fillet wrapped in prosciutto with herby
      lentils, spinach and yoghurt 168, **169**
    lettuce: braised pigeon breasts with peas, lettuce and
      spring onions 188, **189**
linguine
    with pancetta, olive oil, chilli, clams and white wine
      128, **129**
    puttanesca 130

m

Maltesers
    frothy Malteser milk 271, **271**
v Maltesers and ice-cream 258, **258**
marinades 192
v Asian 194, **194**
v rosemary, garlic and lemon 194, **194**
v yoghurt, mint and lime 194, **194**
    see also rubs
marinated anchovies 48
v marinated olives **44**, 45
v marinated peppers 45
marinated squid with chickpeas and chilli 49
marjoram
v baked beetroot with balsamic vinegar, marjoram and
    garlic 216, **217**

index

v   stracci with Gorgonzola, mascarpone, marjoram and walnuts 104
Mary's Saturday soup and dumplings 86, **87**
mascarpone
v   potato and Jerusalem artichoke soup with thyme, mascarpone and hazelnuts 85
v   ravioli of minted asparagus with potatoes and mascarpone 114, **115**
v   roasted sweet garlic, thyme and mascarpone risotto with toasted almonds and breadcrumbs **136**, 137
v   stracci with Gorgonzola, mascarpone, marjoram and walnuts 104
v   mashed veg **214**, 215
meat: marinades and rubs for 192–5
midnight pan-cooked breakfast **26**, 27
milk, frothy Malteser 271, **271**
mint
   mixed leaf salad with mozzarella, mint, peach and prosciutto 68, **69**
   prawn and pea risotto with basil and mint 142, **143**
v   ravioli of minted asparagus with potatoes and mascarpone 114, **115**
v   yoghurt, mint and lime marinade 194, **194**
v   minted bread sauce 278
mixed leaf salad with mozzarella, mint, peach and prosciutto 68, **69**
mojito 269
monkfish wrapped in banana leaves with ginger, coriander, chilli and coconut milk **148**, 149
mozzarella
   farfalle with Savoy cabbage, pancetta, thyme and mozzarella **132**, 133
   mixed leaf salad with mozzarella, mint, peach and prosciutto 68, **69**
v   mozzarella and grilled chilli salad 56, **57**
pizzas 232, **233**
v   muesli: pukkolla 32–3, **33**
mushrooms
   mushroom, mozzarella, thyme and spicy sausage meat pizza 232
   pappardelle, spicy sausage meat and mixed wild mushrooms **106**, 107
   roasted slashed fillet of sea bass stuffed with herbs, baked on mushroom potatoes with salsa verde – à la Tony Blair 156, **157**
v   tray-baked field mushrooms studded with garlic and rubbed with butter and pounded thyme 204, 205
mussels
   seafood broth, ripped herbs, toasted bread and garlic aïoli 90, **91**
   wok-cooked fragrant mussels 154, **155**
v   mustard and herb vinegar dressing 81

n
v   nutmeg: spinach with nutmeg and butter 211

o
old fashioned cocktail 266
v   olive oil and lemon juice dressing 81
olives
   black olive tapenade 42
   linguine puttanesca 130
v   marinated olives **44**, 45
v   olive, tomato, rocket, Parmesan and mozzarella pizza 232, **233**
v   spaghetti with squashed olives, tomatoes, garlic, olive oil and chopped rocket 124
v   squashed cherry tomato and smashed olive salad 58–9, **58–9**

v   onions: spaghetti with red onions, sun-dried tomatoes, balsamic vinegar and basil 125
v   orange juice: baked endive with thyme, orange juice, garlic and butter 201
v   orange and polenta biscuits 240, **241**

p
v   pan-toasted almonds with a touch of chilli and sea salt 39, **39**
pancetta
   farfalle with Savoy cabbage, pancetta, thyme and mozzarella **132**, 133
   linguine with pancetta, olive oil, chilli, clams and white wine 128, 129
   tray-baked cod with runner beans, pancetta and pine nuts 150, **151**
v   paneer Indian cheese 190
pangritata: spaghetti with anchovies, dried chilli and pangritata 126, **127**
pappardelle
   with rabbit, herbs and cream 105
   with spicy sausage meat and mixed wild mushrooms **106**, 107
Parma ham: squash, Parma ham hock, sage, onion and barley broth **88**, 89
Parmesan
v   ravioli of creamed ricotta, toasted pine nuts, Parmesan and loadsa herbs 116
   seared carpaccio of beef with roasted baby beets, creamed horseradish, watercress and Parmesan 176, **177**
v   tortellini of ricotta, lemon, Parmesan and sage butter 120, **121**
v   watercress, rocket, sweet pear, walnut and Parmesan salad 64–5, **64–5**
   white risotto with lemon thyme, sliced prosciutto, Parmesan, pecorino and crumbled goat's cheese **138**, 139
parsley
v   celery, celeriac, parsley and pomegranate salad **76**, 77
v   spaghetti with olive oil, garlic, chilli and parsley 125
parsnips: tray-baked pork chops with herby potatoes, parsnips, pears and minted bread sauce 180, **181**
v   party cake 254, **255**
v   passionfruit: Campari and passionfruit sorbet 260, 261
pasta
   dried 124
   drying 101
   farfalle with broccoli, anchovies and chilli 131
   farfalle with Savoy cabbage, pancetta, thyme and mozzarella **132**, 133
   I-Thai fried tortellini of chicken, ginger, water chestnut and lemon grass with dipping sauce 122–3, **122–3**
   linguine with pancetta, olive oil, chilli, clams and white wine 128, **129**
   linguine puttanesca 130
   making fresh pasta 98, **98–9**
   making ravioli **112**, 113
   making tortellini **118**, 119
   pappardelle with rabbit, herbs and cream 105
   pappardelle with spicy sausage meat and mixed wild mushrooms **106**, 107
v   ravioli of creamed ricotta, toasted pine nuts, Parmesan and loadsa herbs 116
v   ravioli of minted asparagus with potatoes and mascarpone 114, **115**
   shaping pasta from a sheet 101
   spaghetti with anchovies, dried chilli and pangritata 126, **127**
v   spaghetti with olive oil, garlic, chilli and parsley 125

v spaghetti with red onions, sun-dried tomatoes, balsamic vinegar and basil 125
v spaghetti with squashed olives, tomatoes, garlic, olive oil and chopped rocket 124
v stracci with Gorgonzola, mascarpone, marjoram and walnuts 104
v stracci, spicy aubergines, tomatoes, basil and Parmesan **102**, 103
tagliatelle with saffron, seafood and cream 108, **109**
v tagliatelle with tomato sauce, spinach and crumbled ricotta 110
v tortellini of ricotta, lemon, Parmesan and sage butter 120, **121**
peaches
Bellini 267
mixed leaf salad with mozzarella, mint, peach and prosciutto 68, **69**
roast loin of pork with peaches 172, **173**
v Sheila's pudding 252, **253**
pears
tray-baked pork chops with herby potatoes, parsnips, pears and minted bread sauce 180, **181**
v watercress, rocket, sweet pear, walnut and Parmesan salad 64–5, **64–5**
peas
braised pigeon breasts with peas, lettuce and spring onions 188, **189**
prawn and pea risotto with basil and mint 142, **143**
v spring onions, sweet peas, white wine and spinach 212, **213**
pecorino: white risotto with lemon thyme, sliced prosciutto, pecorino and crumbled goat's cheese 138, **139**
v peppers: blackened marinated peppers 45
Peter's lamb curry 190, **191**
pigeon: braised pigeon breasts with peas, lettuce and spring onions 188, 189
pine nuts
v basil, balsamic and pine nut dressing 80
v ravioli of creamed ricotta, toasted pine nuts, Parmesan and loadsa herbs 116
tray-baked cod with runner beans, pancetta and pine nuts 150, **151**
pineapple
blackberry and pineapple smoothie 272, **273**
v pineapple and grapefruit frappé 261
pizzas
mozzarella, prosciutto and basil 232
mushroom, mozzarella, thyme and spicy sausage meat 232
v olive, tomato, rocket, Parmesan and mozzarella 232, **233**
v polenta: orange and polenta biscuits **240**, 241
v pomegranates: celery, celeriac, parsley and pomegranate salad **76**, 77
porcini
roasted fillet of beef rolled in herbs and porcini and wrapped in prosciutto 186, **187**
v spinach and porcini with rosemary and lemon 211
pork
roast loin of pork with peaches 172, **173**
tray-baked pork chops with herby potatoes, parsnips, pears and minted bread sauce 180, **181**
v Portuguese custard pie 246–9, **246**, **249**
potato(es)
baked trout and potatoes with a crème fraîche, walnut and horseradish sauce **162**, 163
v potato and Jerusalem artichoke soup with thyme, mascarpone and hazelnuts 85

v ravioli of minted asparagus with potatoes and mascarpone 114, **115**
roasted Hamilton poussin wrapped with streaky bacon and stuffed with potatoes and sage 182, **183**
roasted slashed fillet of sea bass stuffed with herbs, baked on mushroom potatoes with salsa verde – à la Tony Blair 156, **157**
v salad of boiled potatoes, avocado and cress 70, **71**
tray-baked pork chops with herby potatoes, parsnips, pears and minted bread sauce 180, **181**
prawn(s)
fragrant Thai broth 92, **93**
prawn and pea risotto with basil and mint 142, **143**
salted and spiced prawns 49
prosciutto
Gennaro bread **230**, 231
mixed leaf salad with mozzarella, mint, peach and prosciutto 68, **69**
mozzarella, prosciutto and basil pizza 232
roasted fillet of beef rolled in herbs and porcini and wrapped in prosciutto 186, **187**
salmon fillet wrapped in prosciutto with herby lentils, spinach and yoghurt 168, **169**
seared scallops and crispy prosciutto with roasted tomatoes and smashed white beans 160, **161**
white risotto with lemon thyme, sliced prosciutto, pecorino and crumbled goat's cheese 138, **139**
v pukkolla 32–3, **33**

r
rabbit: pappardelle with rabbit, herbs and cream 105
radicchio: risotto of radicchio, smoky bacon, rosemary and red wine 144, **145**
radishes: seared carpaccio of beef with chilli, ginger, radish and soy **178**, 179
raspberry and strawberry smoothie 272, **273**
ravioli
making **112**, 113
v ravioli of creamed ricotta, toasted pine nuts, Parmesan and loadsa herbs 116
v ravioli of minted asparagus with potatoes and mascarpone 114, **115**
red wine: risotto of radicchio, smoky bacon, rosemary and red wine 144, **145**
rice
v steamed spinach with coconut rice 212
see also risotto
ricotta
v figs, honey and ricotta 28, **29**
v ravioli of creamed ricotta, toasted pine nuts, Parmesan and loadsa herbs 116
v tagliatelle with tomato sauce, spinach and crumbled ricotta 110
v tortellini of ricotta, lemon, Parmesan and sage butter 120, **121**
risotto
v basic recipe 134-5, **135**
prawn and pea risotto with basil and mint 142, **143**
risotto of radicchio, smoky bacon, rosemary and red wine 144, **145**
v roasted sweet garlic, thyme and mascarpone risotto with toasted almonds and breadcrumbs 136, **137**
white risotto with lemon thyme, sliced prosciutto, pecorino and crumbled goat's cheese 138, **139**
roasted chicken, fantastic 184, **185**
roast loin of pork with peaches 172, **173**
roasted fillet of beef rolled in herbs and porcini and wrapped in prosciutto 186, **187**
roasted Hamilton poussin wrapped with streaky bacon and stuffed with potatoes and sage 182, 183

roasted slashed fillet of sea bass stuffed with herbs, baked on mushroom potatoes with salsa verde – à la Tony Blair 156, **157**

v roasted sweet garlic, thyme and mascarpone risotto with toasted almonds and breadcrumbs 136, **137**

rocket

salad of marinated charred squid with cannellini beans, rocket and chilli 74, **75**

v spaghetti with squashed olives, tomatoes,garlic, olive oil and chopped rocket 124

v watercress, rocket, sweet pear, walnut and Parmesan salad 64–5, **64–5**

rosemary

v rosemary, garlic and lemon marinade 194, **194**

risotto of radicchio, smoky bacon, rosemary and red wine 144, **145**

v spinach and porcini with rosemary and lemon 211

rubs

v Cajun spicy 195, **195**

v fennel seed, thyme and garlic 195, **195**

v hot and fragrant 195, **195**

see also marinades

runner beans: tray-baked cod with runner beans, pancetta and pine nuts 150, **151**

S

saffron: tagliatelle with saffron, seafood and cream 108, **109**

sage

roasted Hamilton poussin wrapped with streaky bacon and stuffed with potatoes and sage 182, **183**

squash, Parma ham hock, sage, onion and barley broth **88**, 89

v tortellini of ricotta, lemon, Parmesan and sage butter 120, **121**

salads

v celery, celeriac, parsley and pomegranate salad 76, **77**

v couscous with grilled summer vegetables and loadsa herbs 60, **61**

v crunchy Thai salad 67, **67**

mixed leaf salad with mozzarella, mint, peach and prosciutto 68, **69**

v mozzarella and grilled chilli salad 56, **57**

v salad of boiled potatoes, avocado and cress 70, **71**

salad of marinated charred squid with cannellini beans, rocket and chilli 74, **75**

v squashed cherry tomato and smashed olive salad 58–9, **58-9**

warm salad of winter leaves, bacon and Jerusalem artichokes 62, **63**

v watercress, rocket, sweet pear, walnut and Parmesan salad 64–5, **64–5**

see also dressings

salmon fillet wrapped in prosciutto with herby lentils, spinach and yoghurt 168, **169**

salsa, tomato 277

salsa verde 277

salted and spiced prawns 49

sardines, grilled butterflied 48

sauces

v creamed horseradish 278

v garlic aïoli 276

v minted bread sauce 278

salsa verde 277

tomato salsa 277

sausages

mushroom, mozzarella, thyme and spicy sausage meat pizza 232

pappardelle, spicy sausage meat and mixed wild mushrooms 106, **107**

scallops: seared scallops and crispy prosciutto with roasted tomatoes and smashed white beans 160, **161**

sea bass

baked in a bag and stuffed with herbs 152, **153**

roasted slashed fillet of sea bass stuffed with herbs, baked on mushroom potatoes with salsa verde – à la Tony Blair 156, **157**

seafood

seafood broth, ripped herbs, toasted bread and garlic aïoli 90, **91**

tagliatelle with saffron, seafood and cream 108, **109**

see also individual names

seared carpaccio of beef with chilli, ginger, radish and soy **178**, 179

seared carpaccio of beef with roasted baby beets, creamed horseradish, watercress and Parmesan 176, **177**

seared encrusted carpaccio of beef 175

seared scallops and crispy prosciutto with roasted tomatoes and smashed white beans 160, **161**

v Sheila's pudding 252, **253**

v slashed cheese, chilli and paprika flatbread 236, **237**

slow-cooked and stuffed baby bell chilli peppers 46, **47**

v smashed courgette paste 43

v smashed spiced chickpeas 40, **41**

smoothies 272, **273**

snacks

Asian infused tuna **50**, 51

black olive tapenade 42

v blackened marinated peppers 45

v blackened sweet aubergine 42

grilled butterflied sardines 48

marinated anchovies 48

v marinated olives 44, **45**

marinated squid with chickpeas and chilli 49

v pan-toasted almonds with a touch of chilli and sea salt 39, **39**

salted and spiced prawns 49

slow-cooked and stuffed baby bell chilli peppers 46, **47**

v smashed courgette paste 43

v smashed spiced chickpeas 40, **41**

v sorbet, Campari and passionfruit **260**, 261

soups

fragrant Thai broth 92, **93**

Mary's Saturday soup and dumplings 86, **87**

v potato and Jerusalem artichoke soup with thyme, mascarpone and hazelnuts 85

seafood broth, ripped herbs, toasted bread and garlic aïoli 90, **91**

squash, Parma ham hock, sage, onion and barley broth **88**, 89

spaghetti

with anchovies, dried chilli and pangritata 126, **127**

v with olive oil, garlic, chilli and parsley 125

v with red onions, sun-dried tomatoes, balsamic vinegar and basil 125

v with squashed olives, tomatoes, garlic, olive oil and chopped rocket 124

spices 15

spinach

salmon fillet wrapped in prosciutto with herby lentils, spinach and yoghurt 168, **169**

v spinach with nutmeg and butter 211

v spinach and porcini with rosemary and lemon 210

v spring onions, sweet peas, white wine and spinach **212**, 213

v steamed spinach with coconut rice 212

v tagliatelle with tomato sauce, spinach and crumbled ricotta 110

spring onions
    braised pigeon breasts with peas, lettuce and spring
      onions **188**, 189
v spring onions, sweet peas, white wine and spinach 212,
      213
    squash, Parma ham hock, sage, onion and barley broth **88**,
      89
v squashed cherry tomato and smashed olive salad 58–9,
      58–9
    squid
    marinated squid with chickpeas and chilli 49
    salad of marinated charred squid with cannellini beans,
      rocket and chilli 74, **75**
v steamed spinach with coconut rice 212
    stocks
      chicken 275
      fish 275
v   vegetable 276
    stracci
v with Gorgonzola, mascarpone, marjoram and walnuts 104
v with spicy aubergines, tomatoes, basil and Parmesan
      102, 103
    strawberries
v marinated in balsamic vinegar 256, **257**
    raspberry and strawberry smoothie 272, **273**
v sun-dried tomatoes: spaghetti with red onions, sun-dried
      tomatoes, balsamic vinegar and basil 125
v sweet cherry tomato dressing 81
    swordfish: grilled swordfish, green beans and spicy
      tomato salsa 164, **165**

t
tagliatelle
    with saffron, seafood and cream 108, **109**
v with tomato sauce, spinach and crumbled ricotta 110
tapenade, black olive 42
Thai broth 92, **93**
v Thai dressing 80
v Thai salad, crunchy 67, **67**
thyme
v baked carrots with cumin, thyme, butter and
      Chardonnay **218**, 219
v baked endive with thyme, orange juice, garlic and
      butter 201
v baked Jerusalem artichokes, breadcrumbs, thyme and
      lemon 208, **209**
    farfalle with Savoy cabbage, pancetta, thyme and
      mozzarella 132, **133**
v fennel seed, thyme and garlic rub 195, **195**
v potato and Jerusalem artichoke soup with thyme,
      mascarpone and hazelnuts 85
v roasted sweet garlic, thyme and mascarpone risotto
      with toasted almonds and breadcrumbs **136**, 137
v tray-baked field mushrooms studded with garlic and
      rubbed with butter and pounded thyme 204, 205
Tom Collins 266
tomatoes
    beef tomatoes, basil, ham and mild cheese on thick
      toast 30, **31**
    seared scallops and crispy prosciutto with roasted
      tomatoes and smashed white beans 160, **161**
v spaghetti with red onions, sun-dried tomatoes,
      balsamic vinegar and basil 125
v spaghetti with squashed olives, tomatoes, garlic, olive
      oil and chopped rocket 124
v squashed cherry tomato and smashed olive salad
      58–9, **58–9**
v stracci, spicy aubergines, tomatoes, basil and
      Parmesan **102**, 103
v sweet cherry tomato dressing 81

v tagliatelle with tomato sauce, spinach and crumbled
      ricotta 110
    tomato salsa 277
v torte, two-nuts chocolate **244**, 245
tortellini
    I-Thai fried tortellini of chicken, ginger, water chestnut
      and lemon grass with dipping sauce 122–3, **122–3**
    making 118, 119
v tortellini of ricotta, lemon, Parmesan and sage butter
      120, **121**
    tray-baked cod with runner beans, pancetta and pine nuts
      150, **151**
v tray-baked field mushrooms studded with garlic and
      rubbed with butter and pounded thyme **204**, 205
    tray-baked pork chops with herby potatoes, parsnips, pears
      and minted bread sauce 180, **181**
    trout: baked trout and potatoes with a crème fraîche,
      walnut and horseradish sauce 162, 163
    tuna, Asian infused **50**, 51
v two-nuts chocolate torte **244**, 245

v
vegetables
    braised five hour lamb with wine, veg and all that 174
v mashed veg **214**, 215
v vegetable stock 276
    see also individual names
v vermouth: baked fennel with garlic butter and vermouth
      202, **203**

w
walnuts
    baked trout and potatoes with a crème fraîche, walnut
      and horseradish sauce **162**, 163
v stracci with Gorgonzola, mascarpone, marjoram and
      walnuts 104
v watercress, rocket, sweet pear, walnut and Parmesan
      salad 64–5, **64–5**
    warm salad of winter leaves, bacon and Jerusalem
      artichokes **62**, 63
    water chestnuts: I-Thai fried tortellini of chicken, ginger,
      water chestnut and lemon grass with dipping sauce
      122–3, **122–3**
    watercress
v watercress, rocket, sweet pear, walnut and Parmesan
      salad 64–5, **64–5**
    seared carpaccio of beef with roasted baby beets,
      creamed horseradish, watercress and Parmesan 176,
      177
    watermelon vodka 270, **270**
    white beans: seared scallops and crispy prosciutto with
      roasted tomatoes and smashed white beans 160, **161**
    white risotto with lemon thyme, sliced prosciutto, pecorino
      and crumbled goat's cheese 138, **139**
    white wine
    braised five hour lamb with wine, veg and all that 174
    linguine with pancetta, olive oil, chilli, clams and white
      wine 128, **129**
v spring onions, sweet peas, white wine and spinach 212,
      213
    wok-cooked fragrant mussels 154, **155**
    wok-fried crispy bream with steamed greens and Thai
      dressing 166, **167**

y
yoghurt
v homemade **34**, 35
    salmon fillet wrapped in prosciutto with herby lentils,
      spinach and yoghurt 168, **169**
v yoghurt, mint and lime marinade 194, **194**

index

thanks,
nice one, shout going out,
cheers, respect, much love

I'd like to thank a handful of very special people, because without their help, commitment and enthusiasm, this book wouldn't be the book it is today. Thank you very very much. My missus – sorry, the lovely Jules – for continuing to give me slap and tickle when need be. David Loftus, for being the most patient and nicest bloke and the best photographer in the world, and for letting me be godfather to his and Debs's daughter. My best man, Ben, for his friendship, support and indispensable help. Handsome Peter 'Girth' Begg and the River Café posse. Mum and Dad for being mum and dad. My sis, Anna, and new bro Paul for ideas. The biggest thanks in the world to Lindsey Jordan, for being my sidekick, keeping me in order, giving me loads of support and threatening me with violence when need be. You're the best food editor in town, babe. Tom Weldon, for letting me do what he promised. John Hamilton, for equalling my enthusiasm in the design and always thinking up new ideas for the whole look and vibe of the book, and being a dead cool Glaswegian geezer.